AS FOR ME AND
MY HOUSE

Malory Laurent

ISBN: 979-8-9887913-6-2

Dedication

To my amazing wife, Mikerline,
thank you for your unwavering support for over two decades.
To my sons Mike, Caleb, and Daniel, and my daughter Hadassah,
thank you for making me the father that I have become.

Contents

PREFACE

The strategy that the devil demonstrated in the Garden of Eden in order to thwart God's plan for the family is still raging in the world. As a result, it is recognizable that Christian orthodoxy is increasingly threatened. Faced with this sword of Damocles that hangs over the heads of families, the Christian must, more than ever, observe the values of the Bible, which is nothing but the unfailing Word of God.

I would like to express my sincere gratitude to the author for choosing me to preface this excellent book entitled "As For Me and My House." Malory Laurent, my friend, a pastor of conviction, a defender of the family, is one of the few servants of God who preach the gospel of salvation in Jesus Christ in the 21st century. This book highlights biblical values about the family, inspired by the Holy Spirit, which the authors use to have a thriving family.

This book addresses the notion of families in three (3) aspects. First and foremost, it stands out for its wide-ranging approach to family relationships by inviting Christians to abstain from all family models that disregard the values found in the Holy Scriptures. Then, the book offers kind advice to each member of the household, enabling them to admirably fulfill their roles in preserving the harmony that must prevail in any family aspiring to live in accordance with God's will. "As For Me and My Home" is not just for married people, but it also offers guidance to those who are preparing to meet their lifelong partners. Finally, it denounces the maneuvers of the devil and his acolytes while offering spiritual weapons to face them.

As you flip through these pages, I invite you to open your hearts to the teachings of Pastor Malory Laurent and commit yourselves firmly by taking a stand for families that are based on biblical values. You will find tips for dealing with family conflicts, suggestions on the importance of open communication in a relationship, and other essentials for building a home that honors God by refusing to adopt worldly practices. May "As For Me and My House" bring you blessings.

Dr. Jose Saint Hilaire :

- Founder and Senior Pastor of the Church of the Great Commission, Fort Lauderdale, Florida)

- Associate Professor of Practical Theology and Chair of the French Department (Baptist University of Florida)

- Founder and President (Return to the Word Global Institute, Florida)

INTRODUCTION

"Believe in the Lord Jesus, and you will be saved, you and your household" (Acts 16:31). This scripture clearly shows us the preponderant place of the family in the kingdom of God and its very close link to salvation. Although it is personal, the road that leads to it is nevertheless collective. In other words, the way we behave in our families says a lot about our relationship with God.

The family is the first space for human socialization. It is the backbone of any society. A look at the situation in Haiti over the past decade is enough to see that the lack of respect for family values has undoubtedly led us to a societal and multidimensional crisis. In other words, humans are very often a copy-paste version of what they have learned in the family.

Indeed, the family, as a primary social group, must be the guardian of the individual's values, actions, and behaviors. Moreover, it must be a source of change, acting as a container of invention that escapes the most dominant reproduction trends, even though cultural changes, technological advances, and the omnipresence of the internet have altered 21st-century life from what it previously was.

Of course, the family issue has always been sensitive and has sparked a significant amount of debate. However, the 1990s marked a major turning point in the collective imagination related to the family. Over the decades, marriage, which, in most cases, was the dominant family structure and which ensured the legal conditions for filiation, has gradually become one among various modalities to seal a union. The various forms that family and kinship have taken clearly reveal the stratagems Satan has been using to destroy the family.

We live in a world where parents, in any way, cannot count on other institutions, notably schools, for the moral education of their children. In fact, the 21st-century school promotes values that challenge Christian values. Very often, the surroundings of our children tend to take up much more space in their lives than family values.

While homosexuality is an abomination according to the Holy Scriptures, today's society sees it as a virtue to the point that homosexuals pressure States into integrating sordid notions such as complacency towards homosexuality into their school curriculum.

One of my sons was being mocked by a little boy who wanted to caress him all the time in the middle of class. I made it my duty to go and meet with the school authorities to discuss the situation and have it resolved. Following my intervention, the problem was indeed resolved. Parents should not remain passive when confronted with these types of behaviors that may seem harmless to some but could evolve into a form of threat in the future.

Data shows an overall increase in single parenthood globally. Such families are in this situation due to various events such as death, divorce, or the abandonment of a parent. The latter situation, being particularly widespread, carries tragic consequences. In this vein, a child who has grown up in a single-parent family is much more prone to adopting unusual behaviors.

It is statistically proven that a single-parent family is flawed due to the challenges and risks that undermine the child's well-being, such as the lack of parental role models, the increased risk of poverty, social isolation, acute stress, etc. This does not mean that single parents do not have values to instill in their children, but as a result of this lack, the task of raising children is much more daunting. The family significantly influences the future of a child.

If the members of the same family manage to live together in peace and happiness, they will probably not have much difficulty getting along with others. The Bible tells us in Mark 3:24, 25: "If a kingdom is divided against itself, that kingdom cannot stand. And if a house is divided against itself, that house cannot stand."

As a rule, respected communities are made up of honorable and honest families. It is imperative for Christian families to build strong communities, which in turn will contribute to the emergence of stable nations, to guide us to a happier world.

Everyone is indeed born into a family. However, not everyone is lucky enough to have a close-knit family to rely on. Some families are stimulating, warm, and united, while others are cold and dull. It depends on the climate established and prioritized in them.

Added to this is the proliferation of single-parent families, which is far from being a trivial fact because it affects society in all its components. They generate precarious situations, particularly because of fewer financial resources. In fact, the Bible tells us that "two are better than one because they have a good reward for their labor" (Ecclesiastes 4:9).

In addition, family rifts are a source of sadness, tears, hatred, vengeance, and other malicious designs. Women are the first victims of this global scourge. More than half of all mothers raise their offspring alone. Some officially have a husband when they feel lonely. Others are financially and emotionally ruined as a result of divorce. They suffer enormously.

This worrying number of "single mothers" is likely to increase exponentially with the emergence of the feminist movement. Sponsored by Satan, the devil, this doctrine challenges traditional roles for women and men and does not encourage compromise within families. Reinforcing social divisions instead of promoting unity, this sect provokes a rather destructive dialogue within families where women are willing to make no sacrifice to save their homes. The slightest peccadillo has become unbearable. Feminist activists have not betrayed their vocation by opting for separation and divorce since, usually, they are themselves divorced, separated, and even lesbians.

Indeed, families were already under evil attacks in the Garden of Eden, but the attacks have clearly become much more vicious. As you know, we live in a sinful world in which Satan is the prince. Therefore, the hostile forces to the Word of

God that tend to destroy family life and cause much harm are very significant; they tip the scale.

Nowadays, despite the family's role as a catalyst, it is no longer a matter of placing it at the center of decisions. This way of doing things has its effects in the sense that it contributes greatly to the resignation of parents and the acceleration of juvenile delinquency. In other words, the relegation of biblical principles concerning the family to the background has brought us to the brink of the abyss where only a return to the values established by God, the creator of the family, can halt this dizzying descent.

As a result, the global trend is opting in favor of an evolution of the family, which is no longer an intangible foundation at the basis of the individual but a simple passage without the establishment of real family values. More than ever, Christians must be vigilant in order to thwart this horrific plan.

Moreover, the problems of divorce and remarriage are increasingly numerous in the world to the point where even the Church is not spared. The foundations of the Christian life are strongly shaken.

Definition and Origin of the Family

Considering God's Word, it is impossible to talk about family without talking about marriage. In other words, family life goes, first and foremost, through married life because it is the way God proceeded to create the first family.

God first created the earth and prepared it to be inhabited by man (Genesis 1:1). And to crown his work, He created Adam, forming him from the dust of the earth.

Then, He breathed into him so that he could become a living soul. God placed it in a heavenly place, the Garden of Eden, with the obligation to cultivate and keep it. Adam ruled over everything God had created. Thus, he named the animals, thereby expressing the power that God had bestowed upon him. As Adam observed the animals' behavior, a feeling of loneliness came over him.

This story reminds me of a female dog we had at home. My children came home with a male that was almost of the same breed. At first, I was against this idea. Shortly after, I changed my mind because every other member of my family had voted for both of them to stay with us.

The female was going to be pregnant less than two (2) months after the arrival of the male. They bred and she gave birth to five (5) puppies. Following her delivery, I sent the male back to a friend's house. I was stunned to see how lonely the female had become. This testimony is symptomatic of a reality: animals, like humans, can experience loneliness as a result of separation.

However, before Adam himself noticed this void, God had seen the need. With this in mind, "The Lord God said, 'It is not good for man to be alone. I will make a helper suitable for him'" (Genesis 2:18). It must be understood that God Himself had placed this feeling in Adam's heart and He Himself wanted to respond to it.

After causing Adam to fall into a deep sleep, He took a rib from him, made a woman out of it, and brought her to him. I can imagine the feeling of joy that must have filled Adam when he received this woman from the Creator. The Bible says, "That is why a man leaves his father and mother and is united to his wife, and they become one flesh" (Genesis 2:24). Thus, the first couple was born. The first family mentioned in the Bible is that of Adam and Eve. They had sons and daughters, of whom three (3) were named Cain, Abel, and Seth.

The family is the first institution in the world. It was created by God before sin entered the hearts of men. This means that the family is part of God's original plan.

The family is not just a group of individuals sharing the same physical and psychological space. It is a social, natural system with its own properties, its own set of rules, God-given roles for each of its members, and a structured system of power.

In addition, it represents, for its members, the first social and unity circle, a zone of benevolence, of comfort, restricted but solid, within which individuals know that they can count on each other.

It is made of a man, his wife, and their biological or adopted children. The husband and wife may not have children due to their conception of family life or God's will. Nevertheless, with or without the presence of children, it is indeed a family.

Furthermore, homosexual relationships are not families according to the Word of God. Leviticus 18:22 says, "Do not have sexual relations with a man as one does with a woman; that is detestable." The opposite is also true in the sense that a woman should not sleep with a woman. A man who is attracted to men is undoubtedly controlled by a demon. The same is true for a woman.

Abominable are also those who are born "male" or "female" but who, through scientific evolution, change their sex following surgery. If you were born a woman or a man, it is not by chance. It is God, in His omniscience, who has decided that your mind corresponds to a woman's body or a man's body.

Governments that allow same-sex marriage are at odds with the values taught by the Bible about marriage. On the other hand, people who live together and who have children can enter God's plan through the bonds of marriage.

To understand the concept of the family, we must go back to its creation in Genesis. The Bible says, "So God created mankind in His own image, in the image of God He created them; male and female He created them" (Genesis 1:27). Notice that God did not create two (2) men, nor two (2) women, but He created one male and one female. If God had created two people of the same sex, you and I would not have been alive. Almost all the laws of nature flow from this original principle. That is the case of physics, which specifies that two (2) poles of the same direction repel each other, while two (2) poles of opposite directions attract each other.

Verse twenty-eight (28) of the same chapter states that "God blessed them and said to them, 'Be fruitful and increase in number; fill the earth and subdue it. Rule over the fish in the sea and the birds in the sky and over every living creature that moves on the ground'" (Genesis 1:28). With this scripture in mind, we need to understand two (2) things:

1. The verb "to bless" refers to the marriage of Adam and Eve. This means that it is God Himself who has united them in the bonds of marriage. It is as if God declared them husband and wife, which leads us to conclude

that the first marriage was celebrated by God in the Garden of Eden.

2. Adam and Eve enjoyed many privileges. They could open themselves to procreation because God ordered them to multiply the earth. In addition to having children, they dominated all other species.

God's plan at the time of creation is as follows: a man marries a woman, and from this relationship, children can be born. The devil does everything to distance families from God's plan. The most striking example is a man and a woman who cohabitated (common-law union). They lived their lives relatively well before getting married. Problems began to happen the day they decided to enter God's plan.

Satan is arrogant and jealous. The Bible tells us that Satan wanted to ascend to heaven and raise his throne above the stars of God (Isaiah 14:13). He seduced and encouraged Eve to join him in the rebel camp. When the woman replied to Satan that God has allowed them to eat the fruit of the trees in the garden, except for the fruit of the tree that is in the middle of the garden (Genesis 3:2, 3), Satan's response was full of pride. "' You will not certainly die,' the serpent said to the woman. 'For God knows that when you eat from it your eyes will be opened, and you will be like God, knowing good and evil'" (Genesis 3:4, 5). It must not be forgotten that Satan was cast out of the throne because he wanted to be in God's place.

Eve allowed herself to be trapped by eating the fruit that was forbidden to her and sharing it with her husband. They hid themselves far from the face of God among the trees of the garden. When

God asked them if they had eaten the fruit that He had forbidden them to eat, Adam answered in the affirmative as he put the blame on Eve for sharing the fruit with him (Genesis 3:7–12). Thus began the first family conflict and Satan's first attack on the family.

Marriage: A Divine Institution and a Model to Follow

It is important to remember that marriage is the only institution, the only organization of our current world, that came into existence before the first manifestations of sin. This allows us to understand that God created Eve to be Adam's companion before disobedience appeared in the world.

Indeed, the establishment of the marriage relationship is one aspect of God's perfect plan for man since he has made it part of the ideal conditions of life in the Garden of Eden. Today, we must accept it as the divine model, especially because it is intended for people of all times.

God is delighted in seeing people unite, marry, and have children, but He has set the rules to which His creatures must conform while closely following the pattern given to them. If we want to enjoy the wonderful union that our God intended, then we must follow the teachings contained in His Word, the Bible.

Today, as never before, many are willing to get rid of marriage entirely and replace it with temporary arrangements such as living together without being married (cohabitation). Many young people continue to believe that living under the same roof as a person one plans to marry maximizes the chances of a successful marriage.

This school of thought is completely contrary to the model given by God in His Word. He wants your marriage to be a relationship in which he can express his love for you. This can only happen when you honor Him by seeking His guidance and following His pattern.

Marriage is the permanent union of a man and a woman who will henceforth find themselves spiritually, legally, and morally bound for life. This means that marriage between a man and a woman is not a contract that can be broken by one of its parties; on the contrary, it is a covenant made between the man and the woman based on the one that was made between Christ and His church. Just like the divine covenant, Marriage is a sacred commitment.

The husband-wife and Christ-church parallel is noticeable, and that is not without importance. Christ's relationship with His church is founded on a divine covenant. In the same way, the relationship of the husband with his wife is also based on a divine covenant. God's covenant was made for eternity. Marriage is, therefore, a union that lasts a lifetime since only the death of one of the spouses can break this alliance.

The Bible tells us the following: "Do we not all have one Father? Did not one God create us? Why do we profane the covenant of our ancestors by being unfaithful to one another?" (Malachi 2:10) This scripture contains no ambiguity regarding God's wrath against His people because, among other things, many men had divorced their wives. The first witness to this covenant is God Himself.

The word "covenant" refers to an intimate and holy relationship based on solemn promises. In other words, the marital promises exchanged between the spouses are sealed in heaven, hence the seriousness of betraying your commitments to God and to your partner.

Unfortunately, since the fall and the descent of humanity into sin, the sanctity of this covenant has been lost. Before the coming of our Savior Jesus Christ, we were unable to return to God's original plan, for sin rendered God's law powerless. But today, thanks to the new covenant made in the blood of Christ, the power of the cross must enable us to overcome the power of sin and flesh and to be able to live the husband-wife relationship as our Lord desires.

However, it is not a cheap grace that would indefinitely support our journey in sin, the flesh, and all kinds of compromises, given that we constantly repent of it while continuing to endure sin without ever having victory over it.

The new covenant Christian is in Christ, dead to sin, to the world, to the flesh, and to all the works of Satan in general. This absolute freedom, which was won for him at such a great price, enables him to perfectly satisfy the thought and will of God by walking in accordance with the new spirit he has received, especially when it comes to the requirements of the marriage covenant.

God's requirements are absolute. But He can impose them on humanity only if He has adequate spiritual means to obey these demands. Humanity did not acquire these spiritual means until the new covenant was sealed by the blood of Jesus.

This is so true that in the gospels, Jesus spoke most often to the Jews, as well as His disciples. But, before the cross and Pentecost, they were unable to understand the things of the

Spirit, let alone of walking by the Spirit. The Church was not yet established since the Holy Spirit had not yet been poured out.

In view of the universal nature of God's principles, two (2) pagans who marry unite before God even though they do not go to church. God's commandments regarding marriage remain valid once there is a marriage between a man and a woman.

In the various state legislations, a crime remains a crime, even if the criminal is not aware that he is committing a crime! The crime may not be attributed to him in the same way if he is not aware, but it is still a violation of the law. The same is true of God's principles regarding marriage.

Demonstrating the value of marriage and the space it occupies in the bible will no longer be a necessity. This is an important subject that concerns not only Christian singles who wish to establish a home according to God's will, but also It also affects all the married ones who want to understand the meaning of marriage in order to bring their lives into harmony with God and make their marriage a living witness to God's love.

Moreover, we are all aware that we are witnessing a changing culture. In the face of liberal morals, the Church does not always know how to answer provocative questions related to the family. Yet, notwithstanding its opponents in the absence of a solid understanding of the Word, Christians are suffering because of this topic, which remains the foundation and backbone of all human society.

Some leaders do not address the notion of family under the false pretext that society no longer carries values that are based on the Word of God. Does the Bible not declare that we are the salt of the earth and the light of the world? (Matthew 5:13, 14) And is the family not also the foundation of the Church?

Our mission is to defend family values and to communicate transparently on this matter with the aim of distinguishing not only what is traditional from what is based on the Bible but also understanding, through all the teachings of the Holy Scriptures, the message that God wants to convey to the family in general and to the world-wide Christian family in particular. Thus, we aspire to make it a living testimony in a society where many openly express their affective and emotional suffering. Hence the reason for this book entitled "AS FOR ME AND MY HOUSE."

Among other things, the book aims to show young people (Christians in particular) the criteria they must consider when choosing their future husband or wife. The role of each member of the family will also be discussed along with other topics. Finally, wise advice from the Bible is also given to those who want to live their marriage according to God's will.

Chapter I
How To Make Your Choice?

God has endowed the child's body with a developmental mechanism enabling him to assume the responsibilities of an adult in time.

As a result, when young children enter adolescence, their bodies undergo many changes. In addition to physical transformations, new interests, feelings, and desires emerge. It is normal for boys to start taking an interest in girls. Girls, on the other hand, start to take an interest in boys. It is simply one aspect of God's plan that is being fulfilled, the purpose of which is to prepare the human being for marriage.

The little boy has grown up and reached the age of marital maturity. The little girl has matured and is now able to start a home with a partner of her choice. The questions to ask yourself at this precise moment are: how can a young man know that he has found the right girl for him as a wife? How does a young woman choose the one with whom she will spend the rest of her life? How does one choose? In this first chapter, we are going to study some criteria for selecting a partner in the light of the Word of God.

The Importance of the Choice

The choice of the person who is destined to walk by your side for the rest of your life is of paramount importance. Why? Here are several reasons why.

First, choosing the right marital partner is important because of the influence this partner will have on your life. Economically, it has been proven that the success of a person depends on the choice of his or her partner.

On a spiritual level, the reality is the same in that the person you marry will certainly contribute to shaping your character and will be able to engage your whole life either in righteousness and heaven or in sin and hell.

In other words, the daily influence of your companion will help you achieve your goal of enjoying eternal happiness, or otherwise, it will unfortunately take you further and further away from God, the only source of authentic joy. The choice you make will allow you, or hinder you, to love, serve God, and obey Him.

This choice is then of paramount importance because it conditions your entire life. A Christian does not marry with the intention of having a backup plan, such as a divorce, if one cannot have a good relationship with one's spouse. If you own a vehicle that suddenly loses value, you can sell it and buy another one. However, it is not possible to do this when you are married. Thus, the Bible teaches that marriage is a covenant made for life, and "Therefore what God has joined together, let no one separate" (Mark 10:9).

Moreover, there is also no "trial" marriage for Christians, which consists of a temporary cohabitation intended to assess the compatibility of the partners. If one adheres to the rules laid down by God, who instituted marriage, one is obliged to qualify such a fact as contrary to the Word of God.

Yes, indeed, our choice of partner influences more than ninety percent (90%) of our success or failure in life. That is why it is clever to choose wisely from the start.

This is one of the reasons why serious injunctions are read to couples on the wedding day. This implies that the vows to which they are about to subscribe must not be fulfilled spontaneously and meaninglessly. Two (2) men cannot walk together unless they have agreed to do so (Amos 3:3).

The choice of your partner is, therefore, of such vital importance that you should never do so hastily. Fortunately, in that regard, the Bible offers us a whole host of principles worthy of being observed by those who wish to have a happy marriage.

Let God Choose for You

God tells us in His Word that He will constantly guide us and fill us in the dry places (Isaiah 58:11). It is a monumental mistake for a Christian not to rely on God when finding whom to marry. God knows you, and He discerns your every need. Truthfully, He knows you better than you know yourself. So, He knows exactly which partner to choose for you because He loves you and wants to help you.

If you meet a person who makes your heart skip a beat, and you want to get to know and then marry that person, there is nothing wrong with that. However, you must not leave God out of the equation under any circumstances. Otherwise, your relationship is like a building erected on quicksand.

Indeed, in the choice of a spouse, God must not be left aside. Otherwise, it will be a major problem. The perfect God has everything it takes to make your marriage perfect, for He created it Himself. You need to consult with Him in order to get the manual on how to make your marriage a complete success.

The truth is that there are people who live their marriage joyfully, contrary to society's prevailing opinion. To belong to this category of people, you must be able to do your part and, in turn, give God the opportunity to play His infallible role. "In their hearts humans plan their course, but the Lord establishes their steps" (Proverbs 16:9).

If you are a child of God, be sure that your Father has in store for you the one who will be an excellent companion on the road. Hence, before making your choice, make sure that you let God lead you to the person who will meet your exact criteria and needs.

Consequently, you must consciously pray and ask for His opinion of the person. The Bible says, "Do not be anxious about anything, but in every situation, by prayer and petition, with thanksgiving, present your requests to God" (Philippians 4:6). Pray about your marriage and be prepared to submit to the Lord's directions.

There are some things that need to be in place on your end. You need to be mature physically, emotionally, materially, and spiritually.

By spiritual maturity, I mean that you must have an intimate relationship with God to the point where you can hear Him speak to you clearly. Think of the marital process as a walk down a long, dark path where you cannot navigate alone. You need the guidance of the Holy Spirit. Do not be intimidated by other members of your Christian congregation. Wait for God to direct you!

Just make sure you live a life of holiness and walk in righteousness. Maintain a close relationship with God by studying the Bible so that you can begin to develop and identify the diverse ways in which the Holy Spirit ministers.

The truth is the more spiritual you are and the more you seek God, the better things get. The opposite is also true. The less spiritual you are, the worse things get. Take your spiritual life seriously! Pray, read the Bible, and follow God's advice for your life. In doing so, you will benefit from His abundant grace that will also be available to you in all aspects of your life, including your choice of a partner.

Indeed, you should not ignore the messages that God communicates to you in the form of danger signals during the period when you are getting to know the person and even during an engagement. If, at the sight of these signals, you remain inactive and refuse to take them into consideration, let me tell you that your marriage is already doomed to failure.

Such signals are brought to your attention by grace so that you do not become a victim. Usually, single Christians tend to be stubborn to the point of exhibiting terrible unbelief. They often simply refuse to hear God's voice. They allow their emotions to become so involved that they can no longer focus. Remember that Satan, the devil, frequently interferes in situations using your emotions to cause you to make mistakes.

It is human to make mistakes! Nevertheless, there are mistakes that we make that generate feelings of guilt and leave after-effects that persist throughout our lives. This means that even if you end up being saved from the grip of mistakes, the scars they leave remain. The Bible compares a fool who does not listen to God's voice to a dog that returns to its vomit (Proverbs 26:11).

Young singles, you cannot trust your emotions. In any case, they will fade in the face of reality.

In any relationship, especially in dating, it is not enough to open your physical eyes; but your spiritual eyes need to be open as well. Prayerfully think about your options before you act. For the fear of God is the beginning of wisdom, but it is fools who despise God's instructions (Proverbs 1:7).

Before you make your final choice, you must have God's clear directions. Prayer and an honest look at what God says concerning marriage have deterred many from making unfortunate choices.

God knows the right person for each of His children and will certainly direct those who genuinely want to know His will before making this crucial decision.

Marrying Someone Who Fears God

Remember that marriage is a divine institution, a heavenly concept, and God's perfect will. This is the opening of the scriptures in Genesis 2 and the closing of the Scriptures in Revelation 19. In other words, it covers the central part of the scriptures.

Knowing that God is Spirit, and it is He who invented the concept of marriage, spirituality comes first in marriage. This suggests that the idea of marriage evolved from the spiritual to the social (physical) and that the spiritual was the initial model. Consequently, a Christian must have the conviction that he or she is in harmony with the person he or she has set sight on.

One of the first ways to be certain that the choice you want to make is approved by God is to know if the person is a Christian or not.

In the couple, each has obligations towards the other, regardless of whether the latter is Christian or not. If you are a Christian and single, you must be persuaded that God will not allow you to marry an unbeliever. Such a relationship is unthinkable.

Beloved, do not associate with unbelievers. They are not suitable partners for you. The Holy Scriptures tell us, "Do not be yoked together with unbelievers. For what do righteousness and wickedness have in common? Or what fellowship can light have with darkness? What harmony is there between Christ and Belial? Or what does a believer have in common with an unbeliever?" (2 Corinthians 6:14, 15)

This biblical passage is very clear in the sense that God does not approve of a believer's relationship with an unbeliever because you are a disparate team.

The image used is that of two (2) oxen of incompatible temper harnessed under the same yoke, who would work against each other instead of pulling the load together. Although the verse does not specifically mention the word "marriage," it clearly applies to it.

Therefore, we must be aware that marriage necessarily results in a unity that surpasses all other human relationships (Genesis 2:24). This is one of the reasons why God urged Israel not to fall into this trap.

"Do not intermarry with them. Do not give your daughters to their sons or take their daughters for your sons, for they will turn your children away from following me to serve other gods, and the Lord's anger will burn against you and will quickly destroy you" (Deuteronomy 7:3, 4).

From this writing, we can logically deduce that the prohibition against Israel also applies to us, especially since the moral principles recommended in the Old Testament must be considered to glorify God in our choices. Let us not, therefore, lose our Savior by extinguishing the spiritual lamp that is within us just to satisfy our own desires.

The Bible tells us that we should not be mistaken that bad company corrupts good morals (1 Corinthians 15:33). This means that any relationship of intimacy with an unbeliever can quickly become a hindrance to your walk with Christ and your sanctification which is a condition for seeing the Lord Jesus (Hebrews 12:14). We are called to evangelize and win pagan souls for Christ, not the other way around.

Of course, it is not a matter of refusing any social ties with non-believers. Jesus sat at table with sinners (Mark 2:15). There is nothing wrong with having friendly relations with unbelievers as long as you do not go too far.

In addition, you must be incredibly careful about your friendships. Both sexes always exert an attraction to each other, but this should not be a pretext for you to have an intimate friendship with an unbeliever. Make sure that your closest friends are Christians. Do not give Satan the opportunity to evade God's will and ruin your life by causing you to marry an unbeliever.

If you are dating someone who does not accept the Lord Jesus as his or her personal Savior, know that you will be torn between romance and the salvation of that soul. Also, marrying an unbeliever will prevent you from cultivating spiritual intimacy in your marriage. Moreover, it is impossible to build and maintain a strong, quality marriage if you disagree on the most crucial issue of all: Believing in the Lord Jesus Christ.

A man and a woman getting married have made the choice to walk together in the same direction, at the same speed, for their entire lives. Therefore, it is illusory to think of becoming one flesh and one body with someone who does not share our faith. In other words, one cannot associate permanently with a pagan.

In the Bible, we find the example of two (2) talented young men who made the mistake of marrying pagan women. They are Samson and Solomon.

Samson was attracted to a young woman whose religion was different from his own. His parents advised him to marry one of his compatriots, but he did not listen to them. His first marriage was a fiasco from the start (Judges 14:1-3).

Subsequently, even though his first marriage was a complete failure, Samson persisted in breaking the laws established by the Lord on marriage. His union with his second wife, who was also a pagan, led to his death (Judges 16:1-26).

Later, King Solomon behaved in the same way and allowed himself to be led away from God by a pagan woman, Pharaoh's daughter (1 Kings 3:1). This grave mistake led him to take many foreign wives and support idolatry, an action that brought God's judgment upon his kingdom (1 Kings 11:1-11).

Many people take the opposite view of the biblical thesis that a union between a believer and a non-believer is not possible under any circumstances, saying that being unconverted does not categorically make you a bad person. It is true!

There are even exceptionally good people among unbelievers, and some do not understand why they could not potentially make good spouses. Other young people who stubbornly want to find a good reason to associate with an unbeliever push the envelope much further by taking examples such as the following: "But I know someone who married a non-Christian and it is going pretty well. On the contrary, this or that person married a Christian and it ended in divorce."

I must say to those who support this line that marrying a Christian is obviously no guarantee of an easy and uncluttered life. Conversely, to marry a pagan is to go without a doubt to dilemmas, to tears, to compromises, and to useless difficulties.

In addition, there are people who associate with a non-believer in the hope that he or she will convert. Never start a romantic relationship with someone who is not a believer in the hope that this person will eventually change his or her belief. The opposite can happen. The unbeliever changes you after disappointing you and damaging your faith.

In fact, things are quite simple. There are two (2) categories of people in this world: those who belong to God and those who belong to the devil. They live in the same world but do not belong to the same kingdom. We are not in a Hollywood movie where the person who breaks barriers ends up revolutionizing the world. The Lord is the head of all things, and He has revealed His will to us.

It must be made clear that marrying a non-Christian is a sin and that if you do so despite God's exhortation, you will have to pay the consequences of your stubbornness.

It should also be made clear that it is not enough to choose a Christian as a future spouse. It is necessary to mutually agree. In fact, the Bible teaches that you cannot expect to have a cheerful home if you do not agree beforehand.

Differences of opinion on certain religious issues can destroy a family's happiness. Thus, be sure to agree on the place that God will occupy in your life and on the way in which you will serve Him. Have an agreement on the choice of your church and on the type of religious and spiritual instruction you plan to give your children. Differing ideas about doctrine sometimes come to divide the home. Imagine if everyone decides to go to a different church; the beginnings of married life can be compromised, and the children confused.

It is obviously impossible to be in perfect agreement on all issues. However, the spouses must agree on all matters of a general and fundamental nature.

You must agree to build your family on a biblical basis. The spouses must determine in advance how they will raise their children. If you do not absolutely agree on all these questions, be careful! You are going to face serious problems.

Not Being Consumed by the Desire to Marry

Some people are so eager to get married that they become oblivious to the pernicious situations that may arise. If you are in this category, let me tell you that you are playing with fire! It is important not to make marriage a matter of life and death, regardless of the factors considered.

Others are so desperate that they decide to lower their criteria or lower their standard to choose according to the options available.

Brothers and sisters in Christ, marriage does not work that way. It is deeper than that. There is a spiritual covenant attached to the bond of marriage that must be clearly understood before committing to it. Otherwise, there will be irreparable damage. Old age should not be a precipitating factor that causes you to desperately jump into troubled waters.

You must be incredibly careful because marital mistakes can put you in a state of absolute regret. No one enters the fire of marital error and comes out the same. This fire burns mercilessly. Pray that you never find yourself in that pit, in the mighty name of our Savior Jesus.

If you are reading this book right now and have experienced the fire of marital error in some way, be reassured that God's mercy is still speaking. My point here is to help you avoid or escape the fire. And if you have not already entered it, you can decide to never even feel the flame until God sets you up in marriage. It may seem offhand to say that God has not forgotten you in the field of marriage, but it is the truth.

If you have identified yourself with Jesus as your personal Lord and Savior, He has the responsibility to settle your marital affairs, so wait for Him!

Very often, desperados in marriage are disappointed and become less attractive because they unconsciously convey a desperate message. Their facial expressions and posture also change. Doing this is a way for them to speak the language of frustration in their lives and bodies. Is it not better to wait than to rush and burn yourself out?

Certainly, you can make yourself available without seeming desperate. Note that it is not just single women who are desperate to get married. Some single men are in the same situation.

One of the reasons you are desperate to get married is because you are approaching your late twenties, thirties, or even forties as a single adult. Everyone around you seems to have been introduced to the world of love and marriage while you are still wondering if you will ever find the man or woman of your life.

Some people even start to count the number of their youngest friends who are married. They are seriously overwhelmed by the fear of staying single. Do not blindly rush into relationships because of loneliness. If you rush into marriage because you are lagging when all your family members and friends get married, your marriage is likely to be in great difficulty, and in the worst case, it could lead to divorce.

Loneliness is a feeling, an attitude. We do not go through this life without experiencing it, to a certain extent. However, to settle for something less or inferior as a substitute for loneliness is a blunder. There are far worse things in life than loneliness. And by the grace of God, we do not have to be overcome by loneliness. He can transform our loneliness into a pleasant, fruitful, and productive time in His company.

While waiting for God to give you the person He has reserved or predestined for you as a husband or wife, do not give in to the ghost of loneliness. Transform your calmest moments into glorious moments in His presence. Do not abandon the Christian congregation.

You also need to recognize that being alone does not mean you are a social misfit or a hardened bachelor, as logic dictates. Do not accept the lies of the enemy who wants you to feel hopeless. When we feel hopeless, we act irrationally and without respect for God's commandments. Whenever we feel a compelling need to have someone nearby at all costs, we will settle for anything.

Also, recognize your need for social interaction and plan good things. But you do not need to have a date to have company. Reach out to others with interests similar to yours and share your time.

Do you start to wonder if putting your absolute trust in God to bring you the right partner is enough, or if you should give your romantic life a little help by joining online dating sites?

If you do not do things right at this point in your life, things could go wrong. You can say that nothing bothers you, but the truth is that you cannot make a viable choice without God's help.

Do not get caught up by that "I have to get married now no matter what" mentality. Instead, keep yourself busy working for the Lord and preparing for marriage while you pray. The Bible tells us, "But seek first His kingdom and His righteousness, and all these things will be given to you as well" (Matthew 6:33). Exchange your fear for your faith in Christ. Keep yourself busy while doing the things you love. Make new pious friends and do not fear celibacy, for those who trust in the Lord renew their strength. They take flight like eagles; they run, and do not grow weary, they walk, and do not tire (Isaiah 40:31).

Additionally, if you are consumed by the desire to get married, it can lead to the misinterpretation of the opposite sex's attention. The desperation to get married can lead to misinterpreting the slightest gesture of a potential fiancé. If a man looks at you twice, you cannot automatically read all kinds of things in his eyes. If a woman sits next to you at a social or religious event, that is no reason to think she is interested.

Christian singles often like to send signals and then disavow them. Some brothers even go as far as to give the impression that something is going on between them and a sister when there is really nothing. This behavior should be avoided. As a single Christian young man or woman, you should refrain from sending signals to a brother or sister if your intention is not pure and genuine. Never assume that someone has feelings for you or is in love with you if that person does not say so. Wait for a proposal before talking about it.

Not Counting on Marriage to Solve All your Problems

God created love and placed the desire to be loved unconditionally in each of our hearts. Marriage is a natural overflow of this desire. Yet, in this sacred and natural quest for marriage, it is easy to fall prey to the lie that finding a spouse will be the ultimate path to happiness and great satisfaction, that all problems, fears, and shortfalls will fade in the presence of true love. Think again because this is not true in the world of marriage.

I must be sincere enough to inform you that marriage is a great blessing and that whoever finds a woman or a man, abiding by God's standards for entering the bonds of marriage, truly finds happiness (Proverbs 18:22). Married for over twenty-five (25) years, I can say without reservation that marriage has enriched my life in many ways. Nevertheless, notwithstanding all the things it has done to improve my life and expand my love, there are still things it can never do.

Some people persist in believing that they need to be married to put an end to all their problems. This way of thinking does more harm than good to many marriages today. These ideas, both preconceived and ill-conceived, create false expectations that will only hurt your partner, as there is a high probability that that partner will not be able to help you change your way of thinking. Usually, in these cases, nothing will be able to fulfill you, no matter how much encouragement, attention, affection, affirmation, and love you receive from your partner. True happiness comes when you choose to see yourself through God's eyes.

Choosing a partner to fulfill your insatiable needs is a destructive recipe because no human being can offer you what is necessary for true happiness. This can only come from the intimacy of your relationship with God.

The Bible encourages us to live this life for the glory of God, to love Him and others in order to leave His mark all over the world. Although marriage can be a blessing and an incredible gift, it is only a means to an end, not the end in itself.

When we rely on emotional or romantic relationships to gain momentum toward achieving our goals in life, we can find ourselves facing a wall of disappointment with nowhere to run. Marriage can be a means to our goal, but it is never the final destination.

Readjust your mindset, come back down to earth, and let go of the idea that your potential partner will be a savior in every sense of the word. Know for sure that marriage cannot solve all your problems. Only God is able to do this. You must trust Him and do not rely on your own understanding (Proverbs 3:5).

A believer should not make any decisions based on his or her own opinion or that of others but rather on God's decision and guidance. The choice of life partners must be clearly based on the Lordship of Christ because He possesses the life of every creature (John 1:8-10).

Choosing Someone You Really Love

If you let God choose for you, I am convinced that there is no possibility that you will not love this person. You must understand that God is always involved in the ideal marital union, and therefore, it is impossible for Him to make mistakes.

Also, you should love your potential partner for what that person "is" and not for what he or she "has." That is, you cannot marry someone because of that person's opulence. If you have not reached the realm where you love him or her for who he or she is, then do not move forward. The ending may never be acceptable. God's Word tells us in Proverbs 15:16, "Better a little with the fear of the Lord than great wealth with turmoil."

Money is good to have, but money is not everything. It may buy you a bed, but it will never buy you sleep. It may buy you books but not excellence. So do not get carried away by material attraction.

Typically, those who run after a person because of wealth do marry, but they are not happy. At times, they get mistreated and abused. At that point, they may start to look for the origin of their marital issues. But the truth is that those people have previously ignored the problem and based their decision to marry essentially on material motivations.

Dear beloved, look for finer qualities and godly character in a person rather than the size of his or her wallet before entering into a marital relationship. For example, you can check their dreams or goals in life and their view of things. This could give you clues about what tomorrow would be like for both of you if you chose to be united in marriage.

Moreover, the direct consequence of an excessive love of money is insatiability, according to the Holy Scriptures. "Whoever loves money never has enough; whoever loves wealth is never satisfied with their income. This too is meaningless" (Ecclesiastes 5:10).

Therefore, the love of money is the root of all evil, and some people who are greedy for money have strayed from the faith and thrown themselves into much torment (1 Timothy 6:10). Know that it is the blessing of the Lord that makes one rich because He does not follow it with sorrow (Proverbs 10:22).

In addition to genuine and pure love for your partner, you should not give in to pressure. Many people have made costly mistakes by succumbing to pressures of all kinds. It can be societal pressure, parental pressure, pressure at work, or even at church. On this point, young women are the first victims.

As long as you do not have God's approval of your partner, do not let the opinions of those around you cause you to fall into a trap that you will have to endure for the rest of your life. Do not let the vehicle of your life be controlled by passers-by who have no idea what God has in store for you. Take control of your emotions, and never let yourself be influenced by people's opinions; their opinions are not your reality or your priority. If you are not careful, you are the one who will suffer the consequences of your carelessness.

If possible, stay away from people who unduly push you to get married. Always take diligent care of yourself. Constantly maintain a good demeanor, a calm countenance, and a cheerful look. Continue to pray as Ruth behaved while you are waiting for your Boaz.

If you are a believer, you cannot choose someone just for the purpose of having legal status in a foreign country. This practice, commonly referred to as "residency marriage," is contrary to God's Word. We serve a God who gives us every place for the sole of our foot to tread (Joshua 1:3). Trust Him. He can settle your immigration file beyond your expectations. You need to choose someone you really love to avoid the problems that can arise because of the absence or lack of love.

Avoid Married or Divorced People

If you are looking for a relationship that will definitely lead to marriage, it should not be with a married or divorced person. Dating a married or divorced person is adultery as long as the spouse is alive. And it is a dreadful thing for any marriage because the Bible says, "You shall not commit adultery" (Exodus 20:14).

All married men and women who find pleasure in chasing young bachelors are cruel and devoid of compassion. Good men or women do not behave like that. If you allow them to pollute your life, know that the time you spend with them may be the period when God is going to send you your soulmate, no matter how short a period it is. And you can miss everything!

I want to address the young single women specifically. When you give in to the advances of a married man, you should know that most of the time, he is simply trying to fill a sexual or emotional void. These men already have a life; they just need you to quench a certain thirst that sexual demons have increased and sharpened in them. It is unfortunate to say it, but it is true.

By indulging in this sordid practice, you agree to be simply a concubine who can never experience the beauty of a true marriage, and you attract soul bonds. If you allow yourself to enter this mischievous circle, know that not only have you made the choice to be a second-class woman and to degrade yourself humanly speaking, but spiritually speaking, you are creating liaisons that will take years to unravel. Now, you ought to know that God has a better plan for you. That is an original plan for a happy marriage, as long as you patiently fix your eyes on Him.

Some young women of excessive audacity go as far as to compete with the wife, who often believes in magical fetish. Consequently, these young women indulge in deep spiritual and diabolical battles, putting themselves in compromising positions in which they should never have found themselves.

Some let themselves be manipulated in any way by their superiors, while others sleep with their (married) boss in the office. This kind of life does not honor your status as a young Christian woman. Never consent to a married person.

Choosing a married person whose spouse is alive to share your life or kill time with is a sign that you are not ready to settle down in marriage. Therefore, reconsider your choices if you are planning for a happy marriage. It also means that you are not ready to find your own partner since you have become attached to that of another person. You must break this relationship immediately!

No matter how boastful that married person is, he or she cannot really love you. Agreeing to enter into a relationship with a married person makes you a home and family breaker, a transgressor of God's law, His enemy, and a desecrator of the noble institution created by Him called marriage. "Do not be deceived: God cannot be mocked. A man reaps what he sows" (Galatians 6:7).

Prepare for Marriage While Detesting Lies

Everything you do in life requires some preparation. Marriage is no exception to this rule, especially since even the choice of a partner is part of the process of preparation. A marriage without preparation is doomed to failure.

As a result, you should not confuse speed with haste in the sense that you must take the time necessary for good preparation. From now on, at the Salvation Church of God, we do not celebrate marriages for which we have not been aware of the marriage plan one year before the date scheduled for its celebration. My brothers and sisters, a wedding cannot be improvised; it must be prepared.

Define your plans in terms of preparation and fast to ask God to take full control of your future marriage. Conduct surveys with your partner's parents and relatives to understand the marriage history of this family and to gather information for better preparation.

In addition to being guided by God in choosing your future husband or wife, you must show a certain maturity, especially financial maturity for the man.

As for lies, there is no reason to justify them. First of all, lying is already a sin. Secondly, the pagan conception that lies are virtues when it is good is far-fetched. A relationship based on lies cannot survive, no matter how you cover it up.

If you had children when you were younger, tell your partner. The problem is that once your partner has proof that you have not told the truth, his or her ability to trust you will be severely shaken.

In addition, the other partner will start to ask a lot of questions about everything that has been said before, which will put a lot of difficulties in your marital relationship. Some people tell lies under the false pretext of protecting the other partner. The truth must be told regardless of the potentially unpleasant consequences that may result.

You are doing more harm than good to the relationship and your partner by telling lies. You need to assess the impact of your lie if it is detected. If there is something you are doing that you think your future spouse should not know, you had better stop it. Lying to your partner could cost you your marriage.

Do not Indulge in Premarital Sex

False doctrines are raging these days, misleading single people about the concept of marriage. Some say that the young woman must be pregnant before the young man marries her. Others claim that you need to sleep with him to make sure he is not impotent or frigid before you can marry him. These ideologies have no biblical basis, and we must not allow the global system to infiltrate our values or influence our belief about premarital sex. God's Word exhorts us to offer our bodies as a living, holy, God-pleasing sacrifice as we swim against the tide of this perverted world (Romans 12:1, 2).

God wants you to respect the body He has given you and to treat it in a way that honors Him. You must be pure both morally and physically. In other words, our senses must be subject to the full control of the Holy Spirit.

Since you have belonged to God, you have become His temple that is the place where He dwells. This means that you have a solemn responsibility to keep your body holy, for the Spirit of God lives in you (1 Corinthians 3:16, 17). Although you have other responsibilities as a Christian, your first responsibility is to ensure that you remain a holy, pure, sanctified vessel, a place where God can dwell. "Keep yourself pure..." (1 Timothy 5:22).

My brothers and sisters, as soon as you start sleeping together before marriage, you have automatically closed the door to communication and the blessing of God, the one who instituted marriage. It is a sin to engage in sexual relationships with a person you are not legally married to. Those who do so will face the consequences.

The Bible gives specific instructions against premarital sex because it makes those who engage in it abominable in God's eyes. It strictly forbids all other forms of sexual perversion (1 Corinthians 6:15-20).

Notice what the consequences can be when the principles of purity are set aside. First, these immoral people can contract sexually transmitted diseases. Such diseases will not only ruin your health; they can cost you your life, but they can also cause you shame, as well as permanent defects passed on from parents to children.

Even if a person does not contract an illness, engaging in premarital sex poses other risks. The woman is always at risk of an unwanted pregnancy. The man, in turn, just like his fiancée, can see physical changes such as sleep disorders, loss of appetite, etc. This can, eventually, affect their mental health due to stress and anxiety and lead to depression. It can also lead to unexpected financial costs related to parenting responsibilities such as health care and education.

Premarital sex can lead to a much more abominable scenario where a couple dealing with a premarital pregnancy jointly decides to terminate that pregnancy out of fear of what others might say. They may also act due to fear of not being able to assume their parental roles, fear of sanctions from the church, and fear of uncertainties and their consequences. In doing so, they attract even more of the punishment reserved for those who allow themselves to break God's laws on this matter.

When it comes to a pregnancy that is the result of immorality, the young woman may have to raise the child with great difficulty outside the bonds of marriage without the security that normally results from a legitimate union. Every child needs a home in which he or she can benefit from the attention and care of both parents.

On the other hand, some people use sex just to keep the other partner. Some women go as far as purposely getting pregnant, thinking they are trapping their male partner. This is a serious mistake! This manipulative attitude is contrary to ethics and biblical principles.

If the woman really loves you, she will not try to set a trap for you. And if the man really loves you, he will not take advantage of you and then leave. It is essential to build relationships based on trust and prayer. To young Christian and single women, do not give in to the sexual advances of men. If they decide to leave for this reason, then let him do it. I have no doubt that this man will see you for the rest of his life as a virtuous woman.

You can definitely do your best to maintain your relationship with a partner to whom you are not yet married, but the fact remains that you cannot keep someone who does not want to stay. If he stays physically, he can be emotionally absent. I urge you to refrain from selling yourself cheaply by offering sex because the foundation of a happy marriage that will stand the test of time is love.

Consequently, you will need a discipline that is becoming increasingly rare among young people, which consists of showing self-control by making an extra effort to keep physical contact to a minimum. You should not trust the way the human body works. It is immensely powerful, and once it is launched, it becomes difficult to get it under control.

In fact, two (2) people who are not yet married but who are in a romantic relationship should not sleep in the same room without the presence of a responsible adult. They must meet in plain sight. This is possible. God has given us a spirit that differentiates us from animals.

Just make sure you stay pure by thinking about your physical, mental, and spiritual health. It is necessary to break up any relationship that is based on immorality and refrain from using manipulative tactics that can harm trust, mutual respect, and the stability of the relationship. Above all, do not think that the lack of sex before marriage will be harmful to you. On the contrary, keeping the moral values established by God will be much more beneficial to you than being self-indulgent.

Chapter II

The Partition Of Functions In The Family According To The Word Of God

An individual may never be confronted with such important and varied adjustments throughout his life as when he or she gets married because this unique relationship between a man and a woman is a process of adaptation and a way of life that is quite different from their formerly single lives.

While the Bible declares that whoever has found a wife has found happiness (Proverbs 18:22), many married people wonder if, after all, it is really happiness that they have found! That is often after taking the vows of marriage without considering the heavy responsibilities that such commitment brings with it.

Once married, two (2) people who previously considered themselves to be accomplished adults may realize that they still have much to reevaluate and improve. Shortcomings that were hidden in the past begin to be noticed. The person who, before marriage, thought only of the self must now begin to think differently. It is no longer a matter of "me"; otherwise, it will be selfish. It becomes a matter of "us."

Spouses must distance themselves from all illusions because building a happy marriage is not done in the few minutes that the ceremony lasts. It is an ongoing matter to which one must devote one's whole life. If you have understood that you have a lot of responsibilities towards your partner, you will be able to make all the necessary adaptations.

When two human beings start their lives together as husband and wife, they will soon discover that it is not a foregone conclusion because they have a lot of changes to make to adapt to each other. The truth is that each person is unique, from their genetic makeup, personalities, values, natural aptitudes, skills, and talents to their life experiences. Basically, each person has dreams, ambitions, frustrations, and needs that are specific to them. And these differences do not disappear simply because a wedding has just been celebrated. Hence, the roles of each member within the household are important.

Importance of the Home for Spouses and their Children

The home is comparable to a small government. The father serves as President, and the mother plays the role of Prime Minister. The two (2) work together to make laws that will allow their children to thrive in a quiet environment. These laws guide children to live in order and obedience.

Indeed, if a child can be submissive at home, that child will have no difficulty adopting the same attitude towards the people who have authority over him or her.

On the other hand, the husband and wife who live a pious life in front of their children need not fear that they will follow their example. That is because, through their deeds and words, those parents teach vital lessons to their children. The Bible tells us that Amon did evil in the eyes of the Lord, as his father, Manasseh, had done. He walked the way his father had walked, worshipped the idols his father had worshipped, and prostrated himself before them. He forsook the Lord, the God of his fathers, and he did not walk in the way of the Lord (2 Kings 21:20-22).

King Jehoshaphat, on the other hand, was a good king whose childhood was influenced by model parents. The Lord was with Jehoshaphat because he walked in the footsteps of David, his father, and did not seek the Baals. Instead, he sought out his father's God and kept his commandments in contrast to what Israel was doing (2 Chronicles 17:3, 4).

From these biblical teachings, we must deduce that when we are about to start a family, we must have the conviction that the greatest influence of children, in matters of moral values, is that of the parents.

The character of a child is formed during a child's first year, along with the lifelong habits that the child will keep. If the parents are not Christian, their influence will greatly reduce the child's possibility of becoming a Christian. In fact, they may drift him/her further away from God.

However, in a home where God is feared, where love, order, and discipline reign, children learn spiritual lessons that they will never forget. The Holy Scriptures exhort us to instruct the child according to the way he should follow, and when he is old, he will not turn away from it (Proverbs 22:6). They learn to be honest and have integrity so that they can be a blessing to the world in which they live.

The lack of great material resources does not mean that the home is not the place it should be; it is a peaceful and happy place where family members show love for God and rejoice with one another. It is the relationship between its members that warms the home, not the amount of goods.

To build this loving relationship, they have to spend time together. A home is much more than a place to eat and sleep. Family relationships are so important in the establishment of the home that we use the term "home" to refer to the family.

In this chapter, we will see the role of each member of the family in the Word of God. We will also analyze the relationships that must exist between the members to achieve a happy family.

The Role of the Husband

In the Bible, the role of the husband is compared to Christ's love and concern for His church, a protective and self-sacrificing role. It is said in Ephesians 5:23, "For the husband is the head of the wife as Christ is the head of the church, his body, of which he is the Savior."

It is evident that God has placed the husband as the head of the family. This means that He is His immediate representative.

God has also laid down the rules by which the husband must decide for his family. His role as head of the family should not be authoritarian, arrogant, or condescending to the wife and children, but he should follow the example of Christ with His church.

Christ is the head of the house, which means that His commandments are kept religiously. In other words, it is the husband's responsibility to ensure that biblical principles are put into practice.

"But I want you to realize that the head of every man is Christ, and the head of the woman is man, and the head of Christ is God" (1 Corinthians 11:3). This is why we say that by transitivity is the husband who is the immediate head of the household.

The etymology of the word "husband," which comes from the Latin maritus, does not shed much light in French. On the other hand, the origin of the Word husband in English is more explicit in the sense that it comes from an old word (house band), which refers to one who maintains or joins the house together.

In view of the biblical meaning of the word "husband" and the responsibilities that God has given to it, we must specify that, among other things, the husband fulfills three (3) main functions, namely leader, protector, and provider.

The husband as a leader

The word leader appeared in the twelfth century in England. Nevertheless, it must be said that the origin of the Word is much older than that. The word leader comes from the English verb to lead. A leader is, therefore, an individual who exerts influence over a group of people in order to achieve a common goal.

In other words, the leader is one who is able to inspire a group of people and influence them. To take on his mission, the leader must demonstrate a set of qualities and skills adapted to it. He must be a person who leads by example to create a certain motivation in others to follow him.

Taken in a Christian and marital sense, the husband is a leader whose leadership begins from his relationship with God. If the man fears the Lord, he will be able to live up to the tasks God has given him.

The leader is not someone who jumps ship for the slightest peccadillo because he is the one who has to set the tone. Indeed, the husband, as a leader, cannot leave the house and abandon his family because he is fed up with the problems. It is God who has placed the husband at the head of the family. He cannot disengage because one does not disengage from a covenant just like that.

In addition, the leader is a unifier who gathers his family behind him in order to achieve the common goal set beforehand. As a result, the husband is required to accompany his wife and children in achieving their goals as he guides them toward their aspirations and dreams.

The husband, as a leader, should not be carefree. He must be able to identify certain needs of the family without anyone having to complain.

Leadership at the family level is one of the essential requirements that a man must possess to become a bishop. The Bible tells us that he must lead his own family well while keeping his children submissive and in perfect honesty. For a man who does not know how to rule his own house will not be able to lead the church of God (1 Timothy 3:4, 5).

In the same vein, the husband must establish a family cult to help his family grow spiritually. Long before the institution of the Church, God taught man that it was the responsibility of every father to lead his own family in worship in the sense that man was to be a priest to his family.

Since God is eternal, so are His principles. It is always the father's responsibility to institute family worship. When parents and their children meet regularly to read the Bible and pray together, they grow in the Lord but also in understanding and love for one another.

In addition, family devotions are of paramount importance, especially for children. By regularly putting family devotions into practice, the husband shows outstanding leadership because he leads his family to a blessed and enriched path. The members of such a family will thus be better equipped to face all the difficulties that may arise in a home, relying on God's grace and unfailing help.

In order to establish family worship, it is in the interest of the members of this family to choose a time when other activities are not likely to interfere with it. That is because it must be a priority. This can be done early in the morning before going to work or in the evening before going to rest.

It is also possible to do this before each meal in order to give thanks to God because the Bible tells us that food should be taken with thanksgiving because it is God who created it (1 Timothy 4:3).

The Bible tells us that God chose Abraham to command his sons and his household after him to keep the way of Jehovah, practicing righteousness, and thus Jehovah would fulfill the promises he made to Abraham (Genesis 18:19). Given this biblical passage; God asks us to transmit Christian values to our children.

The upbringing of children is another aspect of the husband's responsibility and leadership role because their moral and spiritual development depends largely on the example and teaching given to them at home. The child's education begins in the home. God's Word tells us that a foolish child is the sorrow of his father and the bitterness of the one who bore him (Proverbs 17:25).

Conversely, a wise son makes his father happy (Proverbs 15:20). We must correct our children without desiring to put them to death (Proverbs 19:18). The husband must prepare to correct his children while they are young enough to be able to learn. If not, he helps them to destroy themselves. The husband must put on his prophetic costume to prophesy good things about his family and the children.

It is the responsibility of the leader (the husband) to say, "As for me and my household, we will serve the Lord" (Joshua 24:15).

Man, as the immediate head of the family, is responsible to God and must give an account of everything that happens in his home. Remember Adam and Eve after eating the forbidden fruit. It was to Adam that God first spoke, for he was the head of the family. Adam rushed to accuse his wife, but God punished them both.

As a leader, the husband must set an example by refraining from succumbing to temptation. By doing so, he will help his family overcome temptation as well. He should not look for someone to blame if a family project fails because the leader is always responsible.

That is why young single Christian women need to question their future partner in order to ensure that the man in question is responsible and can be trusted with the destiny of the family that is being built through marriage. You have to take enough time to get to know this man, understand his vision, and see if it meets your aspirations. He must have integrity, ethics, the ability to communicate clearly, the ability to make good decisions, and the ability to manage conflicts.

The Husband as Protector

The Bible tells us of this need that man constantly feels, that of protecting. When Nehemiah wanted to motivate the men who were with him to build the wall, he asked them to fight for their sons and daughters, their wives, and their homes (Nehemiah 4:14). The husband needs to be a protector. It is something that God has put in all men.

The protection of the wife by her husband is the very essence of the family hierarchy. God has organized the family so that the man is above his wife to protect her.

Since the Church can count on Jesus, the wife must be able to count on her husband at all times. She must be assured that he is ready to do anything for her within the limits of respect for the Word of God. Her husband owes her protection against all dangers, especially those that are imminent.

A protector cannot wait for his wife to come and cook for the family while he is at home watching television! It is the husband's duty to take care of the waste disposal regularly.

The woman must never feel that she is in competition with another due to comparison or denigration by her husband. In his social and/or professional relationships, the husband should not be suspected. He must not cause the slightest ambiguity. The husband must not be intimate with any other woman than his own.

The husband must protect his family against his own family of origin, against any enemy, and against anything that can prevent the family from flourishing. In short, the husband as a leader should guarantee mental, emotional, financial, and spiritual protection.

The enemy can be a friend, a sister, a brother, or even a member of the woman's own family background. The husband must defend his wife against all of these people if they have bad intentions because he is primarily the protector of his family. Gentlemen, you must know that you have not been married to anyone but your wife. She should, therefore, be your priority.

If your mother, sister, and brother love you, they should respect your wife, for you have left your parents' house to be with your wife. You must protect your family from any smear campaign.

There are many cases where a member of the family of one of the spouses wants to break the marriage bond at all costs because his or her own has not worked out. A divorced or separated person tends to advise you based on their experiences.

The husband must be convinced that he is the potential fuse of the family and that, in the event of any shock, he is the one who must burn. Christ is the head of the Church. He played the role of fuse on the cross so that we could free ourselves from the burden of sin. Hence, there is a need for a parallel between Christ and the Church and husband and wife.

Concerning the children, the husband owes them protection by constantly supervising them. When you come home from work, you have to go into the children's room to check that they are indeed at home. You must watch over the children by repeatedly asking their teachers about their conduct at school.

Before going to bed, the protector (husband) should make sure that all doors and windows are locked and that everyone is inside the house.

When it is time to do laundry, be sure to empty the bag containing the children's clothes and check the items inside them. When they go to school, check that their clothes are clean.

The Bible describes women as a weaker sex (1 Peter 3:7). As a result, God expects the man to protect and care for his wife, for there are times when she needs her husband's attention and consideration to feel protected. It is in this order of ideas that the husband will be able to behave effectively as a protector.

The Husband as Provider

According to God's plan, man is to work and provide for his own family. Among other things, he has to feed, house, and clothe the members of his family. Because of this, the Bible states that if a man does not take care of his family, he has denied the faith, and he is worse than an infidel (1 Timothy 5:8).

As the breadwinner of the family, the husband must be altruistic. He must be committed to providing the family with everything it needs. He is the one who has to supply the house because it is there that the responsibility of providing for his family falls.

Therefore, the husband must not be a lazy person who dreads arduous work. The Bible exhorts the lazy to follow the example of the ant, which has no leader, no inspector, and no master, who prepares his food in the summer by gathering up food during the harvest (Proverbs 6:6–8).

Since the original sin of Adam and Eve, God has punished men by declaring that it is by dint of toil that he will draw his food all the days of his life (Genesis 3:17). The paraphrased scripture of verse nineteen (19) tells us that man must work hard to earn daily bread until he returns to the earth. In addition, man was responsible for cultivating the Garden of Eden in order to continue to make it bear fruit (Genesis 2:15).

Nowadays, men are looking for women who have great financial means to get married. If you fall into this category, know that a woman's economic prowess does not take away from her husband's role as a provider because a woman who works to help the family is an asset, not an obligation, under God's Word.

It may be that your wife has a better salary than you; the responsibility of providing remains yours. A head of household cannot fear work unless you have a disability or illness of some kind that prevents you from working. Moreover, before even thinking about marriage, a young man must first think of a job so that he can provide for his family.

The husband's role as a provider does not only concern material and financial needs. It also concerns the need for advice, guidance, and support of all kinds. Indeed, the husband must be his wife's best friend.

It is extremely dangerous for a marriage when a man is motivated and attracted by his wife's economic means. It is as if the roles were reversed in the home. This is disobedience to the Word of God. As a result, this man will be unable to play his role as a leader and will risk losing his respect in the home.

I am not telling you that the young single man who wants to get married should not have his own criteria for choosing his future wife. Nevertheless, interest cannot be essentially material or economic.

The Husband Must Love His Wife

A happy life in a home is only possible if love reigns there. In this sense, the husband should, therefore, consider his wife a blessing to him, thank the Lord daily for giving her to him, and do everything in his power to keep her happy while being happy with her. In other words, the married man must take the time to enjoy the presence and love of his wife.

The Bible offers excellent advice to the husband: "May your fountain be blessed, and may you rejoice in the wife of your youth" (Proverbs 5:18). This implies that the husband must love his wife faithfully and forgive her according to the Holy Scriptures. The husband's love for his wife should not be conditioned on what she should be or what she should offer him. He must love her as she is.

A wife should never doubt that she is valuable in the eyes of her husband. She must be able to think of the love that he proves to her daily in the word and deed as unwavering.

Knowing that the love uniting a man to his wife is quite special, God gives us the possibility to live love in its greatest dimension through marriage. For her husband, the wife surpasses all other women because she has become his companion for life. He must, therefore, love her as if she were part of his own body.

We must follow the perfect example of love without selfishness that Christ shows to His church. Remember that Jesus offered His life for us, which is why God asks husbands to love their wives in the same way. "Husbands, love your wives, just as Christ loved the church and gave himself up for her" (Ephesians 5:25).

If a husband shows true love for his wife as he loves himself, he cannot do her any harm without harming himself as well. He will, therefore, strive to protect her from anything that could harm her. He will spare his wife from any suffering and will watch over her well-being.

"In this same way, husbands ought to love their wives as their own bodies. He who loves his wife loves himself. After all, no one ever hated their own body, but they feed and care for their body, just as Christ does the church, for we are members of his body" (Ephesians 5:28–30).

True love will keep the home safe from all dangers and allow the couple to enjoy a connection that can stand the test of time.

Indeed, the one who loves his wife hates divorce and does not see the point of seeking the company of other women. God's Word tells us this in Colossians 3:19: "Husbands, love your wives and do not be harsh with them."

He who loves is patient, so he knows how to wait. He is helpful, full of kindness and benevolence. The loving husband seeks to be constructive and enjoys doing good to his wife.

True love is not possessive; it does not seek to monopolize; it is free from all envy, so it does not know jealousy.

To love is also to behave with righteousness and tact. Love is not disdainful. It must be considerate and avoid hurting or scandalizing. A husband who genuinely loves his wife cannot act lightly or commit dishonest acts that could be perceived by his wife as treason.

To love one's wife means to think of her first by relegating one's personal interests and rights. Love covers everything; it suffers, endures, and excuses. To love one's wife is to trust her while expecting the best from her.

If the tensions and fluctuations of life ever weaken your love, do not hesitate to speak to the Lord through prayer. Ask Him to strengthen your love for your wife, for He is God; He is love.

The more you surrender yourself into His hands, the more He will increase your love for your family, and you will then see the happiness of your home intensify. One author has rightly said, "The family that is united in prayer remains united for life."

The Role of the Wife

A woman of wisdom is one who knows that her role as a wife carries great responsibility and to whom God can reveal the kind of woman He desires her to be. She must be willing to listen to Him and recognize the rules that He has set for a happy marriage. She also learns to put them into practice.

God's Word makes an exceptionally good distinction with regard to the place of men and women in the home. This is what the harmony of a marriage in general, and a Christian marriage in particular, depends on.

While the husband receives his authority from God to protect his home and especially his wife, the wife, in turn, receives from God the ability to support and manage the home. It is, therefore, the husband's first support in his career, his projects, and, most importantly, his vision. In order to be able to perform her duties well, the wife needs to show attention, submission, and respect towards her husband.

The Wife Must be Submissive to her Husband

One of the first responsibilities of the woman in the home is to submit to her husband. Indeed, God's Word gives excellent counsel to married women: "Wives, submit yourselves to your own husbands as you do to the Lord" (Ephesians 5:22).

Submission to the husband is proof of respect for the Word of God and, therefore, for God Himself. It is demonic to revolt against an authority that God has established. It is even identical to Satan's behavior when he rose up against God's authority.

The Bible records that Sarah used to call Abraham "my lord" (Genesis 18:12). The apostle Peter tells us that this nickname was given to Abraham by his wife as a sign of obedience and submission (1 Peter 3:6).

I want to speak to young Christian single women. Do not let yourselves be influenced by the evil movement that is feminism. Otherwise, it would be better to remain single. It is obvious that the husband and the wife are not equal in the home. The husband is the head of the family, and his wife owes him respect and submission.

A company needs to define a hierarchical organizational chart to function well. God, the creator of the family, is a God of order and has placed man to lead the family ever since in the Garden of Eden.

Even if you have a better salary than your husband, you are older than him, you have a profession that is more socially valued than your husband's, and you are more intellectually advanced than he is, as soon as you agree to marry him, you owe him respect and submission because you have made a commitment before God.

Men, by nature, do not tolerate the contempt of women. If you do not like a situation, express your displeasure to your husband with reverence. You must show some self-control by refusing to disapprove of your boss.

In addition, a married woman cannot leave her home without her husband being informed. Your husband may forbid you from certain friendships if he feels that they pose a threat to his family. If you are a Christian and your husband is not, he may even object to you going to church. Hence, there is an interest in not marrying a pagan.

However, the only case where the Bible allows you to confront your husband is at the level of your Christian faith. Your husband is God's immediate representative in the home, but he is not God's equal. Thus, if he wants you to wear clothes that expose your body publicly just to please him, you can refuse. Never agree to indulge in immodest sexual practices for your husband's pleasure because your salvation in Jesus Christ is more important than anything.

In addition, your submission can cause your husband to accept Christ if he has not done so previously. On the other hand, your arrogance can develop in him a hatred for the gospel of Jesus Christ. As long as your Christian faith is not threatened and your husband remains your leader, you owe him respect and submission.

Respecting and Loving your Husband

There is a doctrinal debate among theologians about the primary duty of women. Some say that the key role of the wife is to submit to her husband. Others say that the main duty of a woman is to love and respect her husband.

Rather than trying to determine the primary duty of the wife, it is perhaps more important to remember the place in the Holy Scriptures of the love and respect that spouses owe each other. Without these essentials, the marriage is unlikely to succeed. It does not have a solid foundation. When a man and a woman enter into the bonds of marriage modeled after the relationship between Christ and His Church (Ephesians 5:21–33), bearing in mind that it is the work of God, they build on a solid and stable foundation.

The apostle Paul wrote to Titus to remind him to instruct older women to behave well as godly women in order to teach young women to **love their husbands** and children (Titus 2:4, 5). Because of this, we see very clearly that God expects women to love their husbands. This must lead to submission.

The woman who genuinely wants to obey God will have no difficulty in respecting and submitting to her husband. It should also be remembered that her willingness to obey depends, in large part, on her love for her husband but also on how well the husband conforms to the pattern left by Christ for the head of the family.

Since the husband is the head of the family, the Bible exhorts the wife to address him with respect (Ephesians 5:33). The way a woman speaks can be either a cause of joy and an example to her husband, children and others or a matter of sorrow to all those who even hear the sound of her voice.

The Bible tells us, "Better to live on a corner of the roof than share a house with a quarrelsome wife" (Proverbs 21:9). In other words, a quarrelsome woman makes everyone in the house unhappy. Children who grow up in this atmosphere at home will tend to follow this example and use the same language when they are married.

Proverbs 31 presents qualities that a good wife must possess. First, she must have the fear of the Lord (verse 30). This kind of woman is hard to find, and she has much more value than pearls (Verse 10). She does good, not harm, to her husband every day of her life (verse 12). She must be faithful to her husband. Marital fidelity is an obligation for both spouses. It is precious for a husband to have confidence in his wife (verse 11), and a wife, with all these qualities, surpasses others (verse 29).

Foul language should be banned in Christian families. The husband and wife should not harass or irritate each other with complaints or reprimands. It is obvious that a woman who loves and respects her husband does not ridicule, criticize, or reprimand him. His mood and feelings at the moment cannot change the foundations of the marriage.

In addition, the Bible warns women who spend their time gossiping and meddling in other people's affairs in 1 Timothy 5:13. On the other hand, sweet and kind words, filled with affection, as well as the joviality and cheerfulness of a wife, will exert a remarkable influence on the whole household. The wife must open her mouth wisely so that her husband can praise her (Proverbs 31:26, 28).

The Children's Duty

One of the essential roles of the home is to welcome children and then provide for their development. At this stage, the parents are then called upon to share responsibilities that bring them closer to each other, and that seal their union. Children complete the satisfaction of marriage. They are comparable to the icing on the cake. The Bible calls them God's blessings (Psalm 127:3).

This does not mean that the Lord curses childless couples. While not having children is still a sad thing, the Bible condemns the behavior of a husband who divorces his wife because she has not given him an heir. As for the woman, she cannot divorce or separate from the person whom she blames for her sterility.

If one of the purposes of marriage is to give birth to new human beings, one cannot afford to annul it because one of the two (2) spouses is suffering from a physical deficiency that makes him or her infertile. If you are reading this book and your marriage is in this phase, remember the story of Abraham and Sarah (Genesis 20 and 21).

The Bible shows us numerous examples of childless couples, and in each case, the people concerned prayed and sought the face of the Lord. While Zechariah the priest was in the temple, an angel came to tell him that his prayers had been answered and that Elizabeth was going to have a son (Luke 1:13). Hannah prayed to give birth to a son, and God gave her Samuel, who would later rule over Israel (1 Samuel 1:11-13).

Other families are content to adopt one or more children, and they are blessed to provide a home for small children who are often underprivileged. These children and their adoptive parents show a deep love for each other, especially since they are a subject of joy for each other.

Since children are a blessing to parents, their primary duty is to respect their parents by obeying the principles that parents have established in the home. We will talk about children's duties in the following paragraphs.

Respect and Obedience to the Parents

When we consider the importance of obedience in the Holy Scriptures, it is not surprising to find that the only commandment addressed to children is the following: "Children, obey your parents" (Ephesians 6:1-4). One of the most important lessons a child needs to learn is respect for authority. And this lesson must begin at home.

Jesus is the perfect model of obedience to the Father in Heaven during His time on this earth. He made salvation possible for all mankind out of love for us and obedience to his Father. The Son of God always did what was pleasing in the sight of His Father (John 8:29), and it was from His earthly parents that He first learned the concept of obedience (Luke 2:51).

Indeed, the fifth of the ten (10) commandments printed by the Lord is addressed to children (Exodus 20). Moreover, it is the only one that comes with a promise. Jesus repeated this in Matthew 15:4, and the apostle Paul also mentioned it in his writings:

Children, obey your parents in the Lord, for this is right. Honor your father and mother, which is the first commandment with a promise, so that it may go well with you and that you may enjoy long life on the earth (Ephesians 6:1-3).

Children should honor their parents by respecting and obeying them. When a child speaks to his parents in a defiant manner, ignores their instructions by pretending not to hear them, or hits them when that child is corrected or disciplined, it is a flagrant violation of the principles of any of the Ten Commandments.

It should be remembered that in Old Testament times, disobedience to parents was a profoundly serious offense, even leading to death. As a result, it was necessary to curb the spread of a spirit of generalized disorder and disobedience that would become a threat to society.

If all children respected and obeyed their parents, the disturbing number of criminals we know today would be reduced by more than eighty percent (80%). Sons and daughters who are wise will choose to obey their parents, making those parents proud of them (Proverbs 10:1).

Those who have not grown up in an environment where respect for parental authority is paramount will find it difficult to respect anyone's authority. Until the children reach legal adulthood, the laws of God and those of the family's country of residence give the parents full authority over them.

Furthermore, while it is true that having a child is a blessing for a family, God, who gives children, expects parents to care for them with love. The birth of a child means that there is a mother who has suffered. In addition, the majority of parents make enormous sacrifices, sometimes disregarding their own needs to meet the needs of their children.

By following the principles instilled in them by their parents, children cooperate and obey God without knowing it. Love, respect, and obedience are the greatest signs of gratitude that a child can show to the parents for their education and sacrifices.

Parents are more experienced humans than their children. As a child reading this book, your parents understand your situation better than you can imagine. As your natural protector, they are the best advisors you have on your journey. You need to know that your parents are stronger and wiser than you, regardless of their level of education.

Many despise their parents because they are poor and uneducated. I must point out to some of these young people that they are the cause of their parents' poverty and lack of education. In their thirst to give you a good life and a good education, they have completely forgotten and erased themselves. They gave it their all! Their time, their money, their sleep, and their strength were all put on the line. They did so relentlessly and without complaint. In return, they deserve your love, obedience, and respect. They deserve to be valued!

Children who treat their parents with disdain and insolence for whatever reason not only hurt them, but they hurt themselves, too. "Those who are kind benefit themselves, but the cruel bring ruin on themselves" (Proverbs 11:17).

Being Always Ready to Help the Parents

While parents, especially heads of households, have to work to support their families, children can participate in domestic chores. Very often, parents prefer to do a job themselves rather than teach the children to do it, intending to protect those children.

However, the children who have grown up rebelling against authority are very often those who have benefited from too much free time and who have not learned to take responsibility in their homes. A young child needs time to recreate. However, as that child grows older and closer to adolescence, the amount of time he or she spends working must increase proportionately.

It would be easier for a person to take on responsibilities if they were ascertained from childhood in a home where everyone had to work. Young people who are still at home with their parents but contribute to household expenses show an understanding of the concept of responsibility despite their youthful age. Parents, teach your children the value of work so that they can be more responsible in their adult lives.

Chapter III
Family Conflicts And Their Sources

It is important to have sustained and strong family relationships throughout life. However, the needs of family members are constantly changing. Therefore, it is normal for the husband and the wife not to approach all subjects the same way.

From the outset, we must point out that it is possible to have strong family relationships without having arguments. To do this, spouses must know how to manage and deal with their differences. In other words, you should avoid anything that could inflame a point of disagreement by turning them into conflicts.

The differences are not necessarily negative for a couple. It is even essential and vital for family life. In addition, it is important to have differences in life in the sense that everyone is one of a kind. We do not necessarily have the same education and the same tastes. In connection with this subject, the Bible tells us the following: "As iron sharpens iron, so one person sharpens another" (Proverbs 27:17).

If the points of disagreement are well addressed, they will be beneficial for the couple. Otherwise, they will produce quarrels, which are not good.

Moreover, procreation, as we know it, is the work of a difference between the reproductive organs and systems of men and those of women. From this difference, the woman can become pregnant and give birth to a child. Hence the importance of the difference.

Differences do not necessarily lead to arguments but rather disagreements that have not been managed. Moreover, when a couple reaches a phase of maturity, arguments become increasingly rare.

Christian families must not shy away from points of friction. If they are not treated, they will generate frustration in the long term in the sense that the spouse who keeps quiet and takes it in is not a sounding board. After a while, it will end up exploding and causing a lot of damage. These situations should be banned in a Christian couple.

You should know that marriage is synonymous with tolerance and acceptance of each other's differences. If the members of a Christian couple know how to address their differences, they will have no difficulty understanding that it is something that is good for the couple.

When God does not reign in a home, family life is not always easy. Overcoming conflicts, in general, is challenging. Sometimes, families are confronted with difficulties that can themselves be a source of conflict.

Challenges can vary from family to family. All families can, from time to time, have conflicts. It is not the conflicts that are problematic; it is the means mobilized by families to manage them.

Conflicts can arise at any stage of family life. We must remember that the first family conflict took place in the Garden of Eden when Adam told God that he did not eat the forbidden fruit of his own free will and, at the same time, blamed his wife, Eve (Genesis 3:12).

Conflicts are often generated by major life difficulties, such as financial problems and raising children, as well as lack of communication and interference by extended family members in the couple's affairs.

The Financial Problem in Family Life

My brothers and sisters, there is no doubt that money occupies a prominent place in the life of a family and, to a certain extent, can contribute to a degree of well-being. However, poor management of it can quickly become a source of stress and conflict. In fact, there are many studies in which money is cited as one of the leading causes of divorce.

From a Christian perspective, financial success is not just about accumulating large sums of money but also about ensuring that God finds honor in that wealth. The Bible tells us that we are to honor the Lord with our possessions and with the first fruits of all our income (Proverbs 3:9). That is why it is important to manage your money well.

How you manage your finances is an indicator of your relationship with God. Jesus gave excellent counsel to His followers in this paraphrased scripture: "Suppose one of you wants to build a tower. Won't you first sit down and estimate the cost to see if you have enough money to complete it?"

(Luke 14:28). In other words, financial planning is important in God's eyes.

Differing opinions on how to spend money, how much to spend, or how much to save often lead to conflicts between husbands and wives, especially in low-income couples. In other words, money is often the cause of quarrels in the household.

If differences persist, spouses tend to share criticism and hide their expenses. A Christian husband and wife cannot act in this way because it is contrary to God's Word. This is why we have previously talked about the importance of the couple cultivating an effective communication habit.

Even if the husband does not have a good salary, he must continue to provide for the material needs of the household. The wife, on the other hand, in her support role, must be aware of the situation and avoid being demanding of her husband. On the contrary, it is in these moments that we must show good understanding. When unexpected financial difficulties arise, she needs to help her husband make important financial decisions and balance priority-based financial goals. With God's help, you can beautify your home and make it pleasant with the means at your disposal. To mitigate disputes, it is a promising idea to set your financial priorities while adopting new approaches to money management. A clearly defined budget is a fantastic way to determine in advance when, how, and why the money will be spent.

Money is not everything, but we need it to clothe ourselves, feed ourselves, and take care of our families. By rigorously following the guidance from the Holy Scriptures, you will have much more strategies and knowledge for coping with the stresses of financial problems in the home.

Hindrance of the Proper Functioning of the Marriage by Foreign Body Interference

When God instituted marriage, He created a relationship that was meant to last a lifetime, which is supposed to find its strength and perseverance in Him. Over time, he has granted each of us the privilege of understanding the essential elements of a strong marriage.

If human traditions and cultures destroy marriage, the interference of a few people in the couple's affairs will lead to the same result if the boundaries are not defined beforehand. As a result, the families of both spouses and children born before the marriage can interfere with its proper functioning.

Relationships with Parents

There is no doubt that the relationship between spouses (young spouses in particular) and their parents is a problem that surfaces quite often. Getting married does not mean giving up all respect for one's family and ceasing to love them.

Nevertheless, getting married means that the husband and wife give up the intimate relationship they had with their parents when they were children. From this point on, the young couple is called upon to establish their own home. The parents must understand that it is between husband and wife that the most important relationships take place. The Bible commands a man to leave his father and mother in order to be with his wife (Genesis 2:24).

The Word of God gives us precise directives in this sense. We must be convinced that when we marry, we must leave our parents to cling to each other by becoming one flesh.

This implies that each spouse should no longer consider the self primarily as the child of his or her parents but as the complement of one's spouse. In other words, a change of role and a transfer of fidelity from parents to spouse take effect through marriage. The old family ties are severed, and a new, exclusive, and permanent relationship is now established.

At the same time, we are still required to honor our parents (Mark 7:10–13). The process of separation must, therefore, take place in love and with sensitivity. Although we no longer have to obey them, they remain our parents for life, and we still owe them respect and consideration.

Sometimes, parents forget that their married children are now adults who can take care of their own affairs. Knowing that marriage is the prerogative of adults, parents can give excellent advice provided that the spouses ask for it.

However, the parents should never attempt to run their adult children's homes or indicate how their children should go about it. When you, spouses, seek advice, you need to realize that what unites you with each other comes before the responsibilities you have to your parents.

Thus, the wife will not rush to her family as soon as a difficulty arises between her and her husband. She can visit them, but she must never forget that she no longer lives with her parents. Her home is where she lives with her husband. Likewise, the husband should also not stay too long with his parents as if he were still living with them. Moreover, he cannot ignore the meals prepared by his wife when he goes to dinner at his parents' house. In doing so, he does not honor his wife and, at the same time, fails in his duty to protect her.

In addition, when parents become unable to take care of themselves due to advanced age or illness, the time has come for children to return the favor by taking care of them. Children can take them into their homes or, if this is not possible, make other arrangements for them.

Also, you must remember that a seniors' residence or a hospital bed is not necessarily the best arrangement for them. Parents, even in the twilight of their lives, are primarily human beings. That means they need love and an environment that is pleasant to them. In any case, give them the best in their old age. They deserve it.

Children of One of the Spouses Born Before the Marriage

It is not always easy to adapt to a child you do not know who has particular tastes, a history, as well as a former family life, and with whom you will have to share your daily life.

That child expressing rejection at the beginning is ordinary. The stepparent will have to show much empathy towards the child. By putting yourself in his/her shoes, you will understand that the child is not an adult. Therefore, it is imperative that you react with the wisdom that your status as a Christian and your maturity as an adult requires.

The stepparent must love this child as he or she loves his or her own children. It should not be forgotten that this child symbolizes a love story—a marriage that existed and of which that child is the fruit. Do not put yourself in a conflictual situation with your spouse's child. It is normal for a child to claim the attention and tenderness of his or her parent.

If living in a foreign land, a spouse must not object to the other taking care of a child who does not live with them. You have to think about that child in your budget because that is your spouse's offspring, therefore yours. It may be a child you had before you met the Savior Jesus Christ, and the other parent does not share your Christian and biblical values. This should not be an excuse to ignore the existence of this child because he or she is not responsible for what occurred.

In addition, the wife must know that she has a husband in order to strike a balance so that their roles do not overlap and vice versa. You become one flesh with your wife or husband, not with your child.

Sexual Satisfaction

Sexual satisfaction is a duty of the husband and wife, except in the case of illness or some other problem beyond their control. Otherwise, it can be a source of conflict, even in Christian couples.

Adam and Eve, respectively, the first husband and wife in human history, shared a wonderful intimacy in the Garden of Eden. "Adam and his wife were both naked, and they felt no shame" (Genesis 2:25).

Moreover, God's commandment to multiply and replenish the earth (Genesis 1:28) was given before sin appeared. This means that intimacy and physical satisfaction have always been part of the husband-and-wife relationship.

1. **It offers protection.** It offers protection. The husband and the wife must reserve this special moment of intimacy for each other, and they must be convinced of this in order to freely give themselves. «But since sexual immorality is occurring, each man should have sexual relations with his own wife, and each woman with her own husband» (1 Corinthians 7:2).

   As you know, we live in an era of sexual immorality where prohibitions are almost nonexistent. Whether it is in New Information and Communication Technologies (NICT), television shows, or magazines, all relationships are hypersexualized.

   As a result, spouses wanting to preserve their physical privacy help each other to avoid a society obsessed with sex. In other words, they protect their loyalty to each other.

2. **It is enjoyable and expected.** After giving a stern warning about prostitution, the writer of Proverbs wrote these words to young husbands: "Drink water from your own cistern, running water from your own well. Should your springs overflow in the streets, your streams of water in the public squares? Let them be yours alone, never to be shared with strangers. May your fountain be blessed, and may you rejoice in the wife of your youth. A loving doe, a graceful deer: may her breasts satisfy you always; may you ever be intoxicated with her love" (Proverbs 5:15–19).

The sexual side of marriage satisfies the needs of pro-creation but also those of personal fulfillment. Sex is divine! God created it in order to bring pleasure to the marital relationship between husband and wife so that the spouses can enjoy perfect privacy.

When a man and a woman are united in the sacred bonds of marriage, each of them has the right to expect sexual satisfaction from the other. With this in mind, Paul wrote, "The husband should fulfill his marital duty to his wife, and likewise the wife to her husband. The wife does not have authority over her own body but yields it to her husband. In the same way, the husband does not have authority over his own body but yields it to his wife" (1 Corinthians 7:3, 4).

In addition, verse five (5) of the same book and the same chapter specifies that one should not deprive each other except by mutual agreement for a time of personal prayer. Intimacy followed by reciprocal sexual pleasure is, therefore, a crucial element in marriage. In other words, the sexual experience in marriage is a vital com-ponent of married life. It is something good, a blessed and recommended act in marriage in order to procreate, to flourish, but also to strengthen the bonds between the spouses. It is part of the bigger picture, an intimate part of the shared identity of the man and the woman who are united in the bonds of marriage.

Sexual satisfaction is a duty that each spouse has towards the other unless physical conditions do not allow it. For the refusal of a spouse to sleep with the other under normal conditions is a sin and can lead to conflicts within the couple. Hence, it is important to follow the advice given in the Bible on this subject.

Open Communication

Because of my role as a spiritual leader and counselor to the Christian couple, I very often meet families who are facing communication problems. Communication can be a double-edged sword, in the sense that no communication can destroy a couple's life, just like poor communication.

It is important to know that God Himself, in order to create the world, used communication. "And God said, 'Let there be light,' and there was light" (Genesis 1:3).

Moreover, the apostle John emphasized the importance and power of communication, especially oral communication, in the following: "In the beginning was the Word, and the Word was with God, and the Word was God. He was with God in the beginning. Through Him all things were made; without Him nothing was made that has been made" (John 1:1-3).

It is true that "Word" is synonymous with "Bible," but it also has the meaning described in Genesis 1:3. If God Himself spoke to create the world, why would men and women not communicate?

It is impossible to make life together happy if you do not communicate with your partner. In any case, we must communicate to share our vision, our objectives, etc. Living together, therefore, requires a form of communication.

Knowing that the main objective of communication is to be understood, in the context of a couple, the forms of communication are diverse. These include verbal and non-verbal communication, as well as written, visual, and gestural communication. Nevertheless, speaking remains the most popular form of communication for a couple.

"Even in the case of lifeless things that make sounds, such as the pipe or harp, how will anyone know what tune is being played unless there is a distinction in the notes? Again, if the trumpet does not sound like a clear call, who will get ready for battle? So it is with you. Unless you speak intelligible words with your tongue, how will anyone know what you are saying? You will just be speaking into the air" (1 Corinthians 14:7-9).

In view of these verses, the husband or wife who wants to be understood must communicate explicitly and without confusion. Talking is not enough; you also need to make sure that your husband or wife understands what you are saying.

There are people who naturally do not like to express themselves. They do not communicate, even when they feel the need to. That can create resentment in a couple as well as a decrease in emotional intimacy. When you do not communicate, the partner can feel isolated, neglected, or even misunderstood. Indeed, miscommunication can be destructive for the couple in the sense that it can lead to misunderstandings, reproaches, and constant arguments. Such a situation can lead to a toxic climate.

Thus, an arrogant and emotional tone can pollute the honest communication that must be established in a couple. Words do not have the same meaning depending on whether they are said politely or arrogantly because the message is not necessarily what is said but what is understood.

It is a process of adaptation that must last throughout life together. A gesture or an attitude can be understood as indifference when it was not your real intention. You also have to make sure that what you have understood is what the other person has said. Otherwise, there can be a whole weaving of misunderstandings that will undoubtedly generate a climate of frustration in your relationship.

Effective communication requires effort from each spouse. There is a social cliché suggesting that women talk much and that men do not listen. This is why it is important for the husband and wife to verbalize their intentions and to show understanding.

Naturally, the two (2) sexes are not the same. Some women consider taking a hobby a way to let off steam, while men, for the most part, talk less to act better. You just have to admit that in the art of communication, there are times when you have to talk and others when you have to listen...

For a marriage to be strong, it is essential to remove the barriers that prevent communication. Spouses avoid the path of incessant conflicts by favoring a climate of communication filled with tenderness. Open communication, free of arrogance, is one of the essential elements for a successful marriage.

Prayer: The Panacea to Avoid
Any Type of Conflict

Marriage is a three-dimensional bonding that involves a deep tuning of the body, soul, and spirit of the married couple. Certainly, physical union is represented by gestures, hugs, all physical contact, and obviously sex, as previously mentioned. On the level of the soul, marriage is perceived as a union of emotions and values involving the exchange of experiences and the sharing of the tears, joy, and sorrows of life. On the other hand, spiritual unity is not negligible and implies spiritual growth, the sharing of values and life perspectives, and the mutual support of individuals. It manifests itself in a life of prayer in the couple.

That is why Jesus told us, "Again, truly, I tell you that if two of you on earth agree about anything they ask for, it will be done for them by my Father in heaven" (Matthew 18:19). It is not a simple matter of family devotions but of common moments of prayer.

The Christian spouses should see each other first as spiritual companions. They are on the spiritual journey of life together, hand in hand with God. Therein lies all the difference between a pagan marriage and a marriage of a man and a woman devoted to the cause of God.

You can pray for your ministries, for a brother or sister who is sick, for direction before making an important decision, and for your children. There is no particular protocol for praying. Pray as soon as you feel the need. Agreeing to pray is one of those things that is essential for the family.

This does not mean that each spouse should not cultivate his or her own relationship with God. The most perfect example is an orchestra where several instruments tune together to produce a pleasant sound. In fact, the Bible tells us that two (2) are better than one (1) (Ecclesiastes 4:9).

The apostle Peter tells us that a husband who sees his wife as a joint heir to the grace of life increases his chances of praying powerfully (1 Peter 3:7). In other words, our prayers are much more powerful when we agree to do them.

I experienced this in 2020, the period during which COVID-19 was in full swing around the world and particularly in New York. It was midnight when one of my sons knocked on the door of our room to tell us that he was having difficulty breathing. At first, my wife and I thought it was a little discomfort that would disappear as soon as he fell asleep. The situation worsened with the rapid increase in his body temperature and the loss of taste and smell. All the signs led to contamination by COVID-19.

Remember this period, when hospital institutions would take control of patients with the Coronavirus without allowing their families to stay with them. Wanting to avoid this problem at all costs and with the persistence of the symptoms, we went to his room to pray and ask God to heal our son.

Brothers and sisters, my wife and I had stayed in his room all night until all the signs disappeared. This is a victory that God has given to our family. It is obvious that the husband and wife who agree to pray enjoy the privilege of an immensely powerful prayer.

The husband or wife should not underestimate. Prayer is not the business of people who are very spiritual. All Christians need to pray and must-have moments dedicated to prayer. Spouses should also encourage each other to pray. We build each other up by praying, and you can have great breakthroughs.

You have to synchronize yourself to be able to benefit from this amazing power that is in prayer. You must pray for each other in order to protect your couple. Prayer can solve, with a snap of the fingers, what years of communication have not been able to solve.

When a husband and wife draw closer to God through prayer, they also draw closer to each other. This means that they develop closer bonds with each other in a relationship that pleases God.

Chapter IV

Remarriage, Divorce And Separation From The Standpoint Of The Bible

The Immutability of Divine Principles

Modern man finds it difficult to accept and conform to God's rules of morality. This is much more evident in marriage, divorce, and remarriage. The divine principles on these subjects are identical to what they were in ancient Judea and Corinth.

Our great mission is to convince men and women to bend down and accept these rules. Surprisingly, some Christians have the same difficulty in doing so as outsiders.

Indeed, it is impossible to be faithful to our commitment to proclaim the gospel of salvation if we refuse to apply the original laws of divorce, separation, and remarriage.

The most serious mistake in a Christian's life is to think that he can reject God's teaching while thinking that he will obtain

God's forgiveness and will be able to be happy in his personal life and in his home.

Within these phenomena of divorce and remarriage, there is an epiphenomenon of which Satan is the author. It is the weakening of couples, which is manifested by the increasingly common use of the word "divorce," and this generates repercussions even in the pews of our churches. As a result of divorce becoming more frequent, it has also become more acceptable not only in the eyes of the world but in the Church as well.

It is, therefore, disturbing to note that the divorce rate among Christians is almost as high as among pagans. More Christians are following in the footsteps of the world when the opposite should be happening. We must remember that biblical counseling on marriage, legal separation, divorce, and remarriage is both good and demanding.

Speaking of divorce, God's Word is clear: God hates divorce (Malachi 2:16) and that reconciliation and forgiveness should characterize the lives of believers (Luke 11:4; Ephesians 4:32).

The Bible's Teachings on Divorce: The Old Testament Approach

It is no secret that many Christians today turn primarily to the texts of the New Testament, others misinterpret them. However, from the perspective of good understanding, they cannot ignore the oldest passages because they constitute the background.

In the Old Testament, the term "repudiation" is synonymous with "divorce." Indeed, the Bible tells us in Deuteronomy that it was forbidden for a man to forge false accusations against the woman he found to be a virgin, under penalty of being punished. By damaging the reputation of a virgin of Israel, the elders could fine him, and the woman would remain his wife as long as he lived (Deuteronomy 22:13-19). It is obvious that this is a formal prohibition on divorce.

Divorce was never part of God's plan for us. "For I hate divorce," saith the LORD, the God of Israel. (Malachi 2:16). This is yet another verse from the Old Testament that explicitly forbids divorce. While it is true that the latter is not very vocal on the subject, God warns us against this practice.

New Testament Teachings on Divorce, Separation, Remarriage, and Adultery

The Lord Jesus Himself taught about divorce during His time on earth. " I tell you that anyone who divorces his wife, except for sexual immorality, and marries another woman commits adultery" (Matthew 19:9).

Under the law, adultery had to be consummated to be considered as such. But "under grace," adultery is already consummated in the heart when a man or woman internally lusts after a woman or a man who is not his wife or husband. The Bible tells us that any man who looks at a woman with eyes of lust commits adultery in his heart (Matthew 5:28). The law came through Moses, but grace and truth came through our Savior Jesus Christ.

Regarding Matthew 19:9, it must be said that the Lord Jesus repeats the same immutable principles of God. The covenant of marriage is made for life and cannot be broken. In other words,

God condemns both divorce and remarriage. It is not possible to refer to this verse to allow the remarriage of the divorced in case of infidelity of one of the spouses.

To commit adultery, according to the Lord's mind, two (2) conditions must, therefore, be met. There must be a "divorce" or "separation" followed by a "remarriage" while the first spouse is still alive. Separation or divorce is not adultery until there is remarriage.

Remember the Pharisees who wanted to test Jesus. They discussed the issue of repudiation with him. "'Haven't you read,' he replied, 'that at the beginning the Creator made them male and female, and said, for this reason a man will leave his father and mother and be united to his wife, and the two will become one flesh'? So they are no longer two, but one flesh. **Therefore what God has joined together, let no one separate**" (Matthew 19:4–6).

When the disciples asked him about the law of Moses, he replied, "It was because of the hardness of your hearts that Moses allowed you to divorce your wives. In the beginning, it was not so" (Matthew 19:7, 8).

Indeed, if the adultery of one of the spouses were a valid reason to break the marriage bond, both (2) spouses would be free to remarry. Many people claim that one who has an adulterous wife is free to divorce her and remarry, knowing that he is not responsible for the severance of the marital bond. Jesus clearly tells us that a man who remarries after repudiating his wife, who is still alive, is committing adultery.

The same is true of a woman who leaves her husband and marries another. She has the option of leaving her husband for several reasons, but she does not have the option of remarrying if her husband is still alive. If only the innocent spouse could remarry and the adulterous spouse could not, there would be a contradiction and an injustice while we are serving a God of justice.

As long as the spouse is still alive, any remarriage of a divorced person is, therefore, adultery in God's eyes. We must affirm, peremptorily and forcefully, this truth in the face of the tolerance and sad permissiveness that are rampant in the local Church.

Moreover, the period in which the divorce took place does not matter. In other words, the fact that you divorced before the conversion does not change anything. A divorce is a divorce, and a remarriage is a remarriage, whether it was done before accepting Christ or not.

Certainly, our conversion to Christ allows us to obtain forgiveness of our past sins, but this does not mean that we can continue to live in that sin once we have confessed it.

It is clear that Jesus recalls the divine principle that existed from the beginning, which is that a man leaves his father and mother to cling to his wife. This principle remains valid when it comes to marriage between a man and a woman, regardless of whether the spouses are Christians or not.

Moreover, Jesus' disciples fully understood the universal, sacred, and absolute character of marriage since they tell Jesus in verse ten (10) that it is not advantageous for a man to marry with such limitations. They speak of every man and woman.

The Apostle Paul's Teachings on Divorce, Adultery, Separation, and Remarriage

Verses 2 and 3 of the seventh chapter of Romans tell us, "For example, by law a married woman is bound to her husband as long as he is alive, but if her husband dies, she is released from the law that binds her to him. So then, if she has sexual relations with another man while her husband is still alive, she is called an adulteress. But if her husband dies, she is released from that law and is not an adulteress if she marries another man."

Through those words, Paul recalls the divine principle of the indissolubility of marriage to show us that only death can free us from that sacred bond. It would not have been difficult for Paul to say that the remarriage of the divorced is accepted by God, as some preachers and supporters of the "feel good" gospel claim. He refrained from doing so because he knew the teachings of Jesus.

Paul continues his teaching in 1 Corinthians 7:10, 11: "To the married I give this command (not I, but the Lord): A wife must not separate from her husband. But if she does, she must remain unmarried or else be reconciled to her husband. And a husband must not divorce his wife."

Paul is referring to the Lord's unchanging principles that we have just developed in a rather exhaustive way. The Lord's command is that a woman separated from her husband should not remarry unless she can reconcile with him. Paul makes no mention of the possibility of remarriage as long as the husband or wife is alive.

How Should We Treat the Divorced, Separated, and Remarried in our Congregations?

First of all, it should be noted that, for many, separating is sometimes synonymous with well-being. When there is violence, infidelity, and other problems, a separation is very often necessary. This does not mean that the divorced, separated, or remarried person is no longer worthy to serve the Lord. They may have made the mistake of leaving God out of the equation, but that does not have to be a stigma for those beloved.

We must absolutely avoid any attitude of judgment and condemnation. The remarriage of the divorced led to a procession of personal tragedies that were, no doubt, difficult to live with and which caused multiple emotional and personal wounds. Whatever people say, divorces and separations never go well. They are accompanied by tears that generate feelings of hatred and failure. So, we need to be filled with love for those who have gone through such trials.

While everyone expected a condemnation of the adulterous woman caught red-handed, Jesus showed a lot of love by sending her away while he asked her to sin no more. He did the same with the Samaritan woman having five (5) husbands and whose sixth was not her own (John 4:18). Jesus knew that those women did not need to be treated with disdain but that they needed to be lovingly guided into the truth.

On the other hand, we must banish any legalistic and populist position. God's Word must be clearly preached in all Christian congregations, but it cannot be imposed on anyone. However, when the Word is truly preached with the assurance of faith, the Holy Spirit must confirm it in the hearts of all who love God and seek the truth.

Unfortunately, the work becomes ever more complicated in the sense that God's Word is not always preached in truth, and too many naïve Christians are willing to accept false teaching. May everyone receive the pure Word of God with an open heart, and may the Holy Spirit Himself give full conviction to the truth.

Indeed, we must allow the divorced and remarried to be fully convinced of the truth under the guidance of the Word of God and the Holy Spirit. One of the missions of the Holy Spirit is to convince the Christian and to teach him about sin and righteousness by leading him to the truth. In principle, a child of God is a supporter of the truth; he does not want to be led by lies.

We can trust that the Lord's sheep will always eventually hear his voice. Hence, they must ardently desire to know the truth and ask God for discernment in order to enable His word to free them from all false doctrine and false teaching.

Some false beliefs are so embedded that they cause some people in violation of God's Word to have an awful attitude toward the gospel of salvation. The Lord must be given time to reveal the truth. Some may immediately realize that the life they live is not in accordance with God's requirements; others need much more time.

If you are reading this book and you are experiencing such a situation, know that you are being called to seek reconciliation with your husband or wife as much as possible with God's help. Nothing is impossible for one who believes (Mark 9:23).

How to Avoid Divorce

The first way to avoid divorce is to submit to God's Word. We know that God is at the origin of marriage. So He knows what works and what does not. He knows what makes us grow and what destroys us, what makes a relationship successful, and what poisons it. Essentially, He knows the heart of the partner He has predestined for you! He has given us, in the Holy Scriptures, all the principles we need for our marriages to be happy and lasting.

Therefore, we must reject divorce as an option. In some European countries, when a newly married couple enters their home for the first time, they go through a special door. After they have passed, this door is locked and no longer used until one of the two spouses dies and the body is taken out.

In the way the Bible describes marriage, it bears an uncanny resemblance to such a house. Once a man and a woman enter into marriage, the door of their commitment should be resolutely closed so that it never opens again until the man or woman passes from life to death. It is in this perspective that the famous marriage vows are repeated: "Until death do us part." Unfortunately, many couples are unable to keep that door shut.

Marriage is a commitment. It is, therefore, necessary that this commitment be absolute. The husband and wife promise to stay together no matter what. We must detest divorce and not consider it as an option. If you enter marriage with an exit option in mind, the time will come when you will be tempted to use it. Once you accept the possibility of divorce, the marriage is in jeopardy.

Infidelity: A Cause of Separation and Divorce

Marriage is not only a lifelong commitment of a man and a woman who share their identity, but it also calls for the fidelity of both spouses. They are required to be faithful to each other. The Holy Scriptures make no concessions in this matter. The husband owes fidelity to his wife and the wife to her husband. "Marriage should be honored by all, and the marriage bed kept pure, for God will judge the adulterer and all the sexually immoral" (Hebrews 13:4).

The Bible does not compromise in this area, and it is clear that polygamy is of the devil. The apostle Paul told Titus to command older women to tutor younger women in the church "for the purpose of teaching young women to love their husbands and children" (Titus 2:3, 4). When a woman marries, she commits to give herself only to her husband. The husband also owes her fidelity and protection.

For the honor of the marriage and for the health of the couple, the Bible strictly forbids any adulterous relationship. This is the seventh commandment proclaimed on Mount Sinai. "Thou shalt not commit adultery" (Exodus 20:14). Jesus mentioned this commandment in His conversation with the rich young man (Matthew 19:18). In his list of the sins of the flesh, Paul first mentioned fornication, of which adultery is a form (Galatians 5:18-20).

Fidelity in marriage is the materialization of the vows pronounced before God and before society during the marriage ceremony: "I promise to be faithful to you." To remain faithful, spouses must love each other, a profound love that does not depend on happiness or any outward sign of success.

Fidelity in a couple has many advantages. Here are some of them:

1. By remaining faithful, the spouses will keep their hearts for one another.

2. They will keep their promise of loyalty.

3. They will not seek their well-being in anyone other than their spouse.

4. They do not give the devil any possibility of interfering through another person.

5. They protect themselves against a number of sexually transmitted diseases.

Nowadays, there are many young people who think that fidelity is something disconnected from reality in the sense that it is reserved for a few extraordinary people. In some parts of the world, the rate of infidelity in marriage is close to fifty percent (50%). God requires fidelity in the couple so that we can have a strong and serious lifestyle.

Human flesh has a sad inclination not to keep God's commandments. As a result, we can do nothing without the help of our Savior Jesus. God is the first to commit and promise to accompany us throughout our lives.

According to the new norms of contemporary development, absolute fidelity is not natural. Of course not, because we live in a fallen world. However, for our first parents in the earthly Paradise, it was the most natural thing in the world. In modern times, it is part of every solid and happy marriage.

Conclusion

Ultimately, it must be remembered that marriage is Divine! Everything was predetermined and decided in heaven. The Bible says that everything that God has created was good. In the case of man, God has seen that it was not good for man to be alone. So He gave him a helper like him.

The first marital relationship began when God brought the woman to the man. As husband and wife, Adam and Eve enjoyed the wonderful Garden of Eden that God had created for them.

Human nature remained the same as that of the first couple after the fall. All men have the same sinful tendencies that can lead to the same delusions.

Moreover, Satan is still the great deceiver and murderer that he has been from the Garden of Eden. Consequently, he tries to corrupt what God has given to man as a blessing. This particularly concerns married life and family life.

Society offers few answers to turn the tide and thus allow unhappy couples to get back on their feet. Yet the answers are to be found in the most widely published book of all human history: the Bible.

For a marriage to conform to God's plan, the husband and wife must necessarily have an incredibly good relationship with Him. Remember that He is the one who created marriage. The serious difficulties you face in your family are undoubtedly the consequence of the Lord being sidelined in the equation of your marriage.

Fortunately, it is not all over! You can go back to your creator by acknowledging that you have gotten yourself into trouble and cannot get by without Him. Also, recognize that your personal relationship with God can be the foundation of a strong marriage.

If you are reading this book and are not yet married, I tell you once again you are lucky! You must observe biblical principles to make your choice wisely. You should never choose someone who does not have the fear of God. This is the basis of the relationship.

Make sure you get the green light from God on the person you are setting your sight on. Prayer is the most effective way to know how to recognize and choose the person God has reserved for you. Do not ignore the warning and danger signals.

You must be willing to seek your future wife or husband solely in Christ and in Him alone. Thus, you must trust God. That requires patience, fellowship, a life of relentless prayer, total submission to His wise counsels, and unwavering faith to accept and do His will.

While waiting for your life partner, you should refrain from being desperate. Your age should not be a burden or a precipitating factor for you. What is fast for you can be slow for God. The opposite is also true. He will give you the partner of your life at the right time.

You must be motivated and guided first by love. This is what will allow you to get through the most complicated gridlocks in your life as a couple. True love is respectful, patient, and tolerant. A relationship in which the sentimental foundation is not love and the spiritual foundation is not the fear of God is doomed to failure.

Furthermore, you must show a certain purity, especially on the sexual level, while waiting for God to tell you the person who is destined to be your life companion. Your body is the temple of the Holy Spirit. You must respect this body so that God may always be glorified and honored through it.

The guidelines are in the Bible, and you must distinguish between the world standards of marriage and divine principles. While the Scripture rejects all sexual relations outside of marriage, global norms accept cohabitation and premarital sex as a normal way of life.

You who are already married know that God has entrusted you with one of the special functions. In that sense, the husband represents the leader, protector, and provider of the family. He ensures that everything needed for the well-being of his family is provided. His role is comparable to that of a company manager.

It is the husband who has to work to provide for his family and solve the problems of his household. This is one of the reasons why the role of the husband in the Bible is compared to Christ's love and concern for His church.

If the stresses of daily life ever arise in the home, it is the husband's primary responsibility to consult God about his family. A good husband is a man who has an exceptionally good relationship with God.

The children's education is, without a doubt, one of the important aspects of responsibility. In achieving this, the husband fully assumes his role as a leader and spiritual provider for his family. He must be responsible for teaching his children the importance of reading and meditating on the Word of God, instituting family devotions, orienting the family towards fundamentally Christian values, and having a vision of life for the family.

The husband must love his wife too. Before being a father, he must know that he is a husband. Thus, a man who loves his wife will regularly compliment her. The husband must create moments of leisure, which can be periods of vacation or family outings. This greatly contributes to the well-being and development of a family.

The woman, on the other hand, must submit, love, and respect her husband, who is her leader. God has placed the husband as the head of the family regardless of his status and his material or financial means. Indeed, a woman who disapproves of her husband shows no respect for the Lord.

I want to speak to married women in general but Christian women, in particular, to tell you that you should speak to your husband with reverence. Naturally, men do not like it when women stand up to them. If you are not willing to submit to God's immediate representative in the family, do not marry!

When a woman takes the path of marriage, she gives her husband the power to decide for her because the husband is in charge. This does not mean that women do not have a say in the decisions that must be made to ensure the proper functioning of the household. However, the leadership of the family was not entrusted to her.

She has to watch over her husband. For example, check if his nails are maintained, especially if your husband is of the "I don't care" type. The wife has to make sure that his tie fits well and that there is harmony in the colors that he wears. I can imagine the pride of a woman whose husband is well-dressed due to her efforts. Ladies, those small adjustments that you think of as minor details can make a significant difference.

The wife is also responsible for raising the children with her husband. Remember, the apostle Paul articulated that Timothy's faith was the result of his mother's teaching (2 Timothy 1:5). Like the husband, the wife must also be a role model for her children.

It is true that the school and the Church contribute to the education of a child to a certain extent. However, nothing compares to the education the child receives at home.

Absolutely, parents must teach their children to take care of their bodies. Early on, a child must learn the importance of developing good habits, brushing the teeth at least twice a day, washing frequently, and dressing decently.

When it comes to children, God commands them to be obedient to their parents if they want to be happy and live long. A respectful child does not speak to his or her parents in a rude way and makes sure to carry out their orders. The child must be obedient.

Respect for authority is essential for a child. That leads them to become respectable citizens. Parents must show their children the importance of acting within boundaries.

From an early age, a child can perform some daily household chores with the help of their parents. However, knowing that the work must adapt to that child's age. A child is not a maid, a babysitter, or a gardener.

Children should strive to bring honor to their families by behaving in a way that is worthy of a Christian family. If all children had obeyed their parents, juvenile delinquency and the prison population would be considerably reduced.

Children must love their parents and must be willing to show them gratitude. Additionally, the parents must be honored and respected. It is by obeying, loving, and respecting them that a child can thank the parents for their love and care.

Moreover, despite the union of the woman and the man in the bonds of marriage, they remain two (2) individuals who do not always share the same opinions. Husbands and wives, you must appreciate your differences because they can bring about good things. This is evidenced by the privilege of two different individuals conceiving and giving birth to a child.

Your differences must be understood and accepted in an atmosphere of mutual respect so as not to cause frustration on both sides. At this stage, we no longer speak of difference but of "conflict." The sources of conflict can be diverse. This could include a misunderstanding, a miscommunication, or a problem with finances. Regardless of the cause, a couple should not play with conflict. Otherwise, it can lead to major problems. And if it becomes chronic, it can destroy the foundations of your family. Open and effective communication is also necessary to clear out your disputes.

Prayer remains the ultimate remedy to help you overcome everything. Husband and wife should pray together if they want their prayers to be more powerful.

Divorce should never be considered an option if the marriage does not work out. A Christian should despise divorce, for God Himself hates divorce, and immutability is an integral part of God's character. He will never change!

Marriage is a blessing from God. No one should separate what God has joined. Someone once said, "Marriage is not so much about finding the right spouse as it is about being the right spouse." You should also know that a remarriage is synonymous with adultery if the other spouse is still alive.

Divorce, extramarital affairs (infidelity), and marriage counseling are some of the ways people try to overcome troubled marriages. However, you may realize that these remedies can make the situation worse than it previously was.

You who are troubled by what has become of your marriage, you for whom reconciliation seems impossible, turn to God, the architect of marriage, the one who knows your problems and offers the solution.

Therefore, you will no longer allow Satan the devil to lodge in your home. As you apply biblical counsel, you will experience happiness in your family. And you will then be able to say powerfully, "**As for me and my house**, we will serve the Lord."

Bibliography

La Bible du Semeur

La Bible Thompson

La Sainte Bible avec les commentaires de John MacArthur

La Sainte Bible Esprit et Vie

La Sainte Bible Scofield

Henri VIAUD-MURAT La famille chrétienne selon la Bible

Brian et Cara CROFT La famille du pasteur

H. WITS La famille selon le plan de Dieu

Peterson OMOJA ABU Le bon choix pour le mariage

Rex JACKSON Le mariage et le foyer chrétien